Anonymous

Proceedings at the Dedication of the Soldiers' and Sailors'

Monument, in Providence,

to which is appended a list of the deceased soldiers and sailors whose

names are sculptured upon the monument. Vol. 1

Anonymous

Proceedings at the Dedication of the Soldiers' and Sailors' Monument, in Providence,
to which is appended a list of the deceased soldiers and sailors whose names are sculptured upon the monument. Vol. 1

ISBN/EAN: 9783337307806

Printed in Europe, USA, Canada, Australia, Japan

Cover: Foto ©ninafisch / pixelio.de

More available books at **www.hansebooks.com**

PROCEEDINGS

AT THE

DEDICATION

OF THE

Soldiers' and Sailors'

MONUMENT,

IN PROVIDENCE,

TO WHICH IS APPENDED A LIST OF THE DECEASED SOLDIERS AND
SAILORS WHOSE NAMES ARE SCULPTURED UPON THE
MONUMENT.

PROVIDENCE:
A. CRAWFORD GREENE, PRINTER TO THE STATE.
1871.

PROCEEDINGS.

The General Assembly having appointed Saturday, the 16th of September, 1871, as the day on which the Dedication of the Soldiers' and Sailors' Monument should take place, the State Committee took every means in their power to provide for the accommodation of the families and relatives of the deceased soldiers and sailors to whose memory the Monument had been erected. A platform was raised on three sides of the Monument with seats sufficient to accommodate about twenty-three hundred persons, including the invited guests. Great pains were taken to furnish tickets through agents appointed for the purpose, to families of deceased soldiers and sailors in all parts of the State, and all who applied received them.

The annual muster of the Militia was suspended by order of the Governor, and all the uniformed companies in the State were required to appear in Providence on the 16th of September, to take part in the proceedings attending the Dedication.

To provide for the Veterans who had served in the War and the uniformed Militia of the State, the whole of the large square known as Exchange Place, was enclosed and guarded by a large body of policemen.

In addition to the families of the deceased Soldiers and Sailors, the following gentlemen were seated on the platform :

His Excellency Governor Padelford, the Rhode Island Delegation in Congress, Members of the Diplomatic Corps, Officers of the Army and Navy, the Governors of the New England States, Judges of the Supreme Court and Court of Common Pleas, the Mayors of the Cities of Newport and Providence, Mr. Randolph Rogers, the Sculptor, and Mr. J. G. Batterson, the Architect of the Monument, the State Officers, the Aldermen and Common Council of the City of Newport, the Aldermen and Common Council of the City of Providence, the President and Professors of Brown University, the Lieutenant-Governor, and Members of the General Assembly, the State Committee on the Monument, the Presidents of the several Town Councils, and Town Clerks, with other invited guests.

A choir of upwards of three hundred singers under the direction of Edwin Barker, Esq., had places on rising seats above the platform.

The Civic Marshals in attendance on the platform and around the Monument to receive the Soldiers families and other invited guests, were as follows :

Robert Grosvenor, *Chief Civic Marshal.*

Assistants.—Charles P. Robinson, William G. Nightingale, Lewis T. Foster, E. W. Mason, William L. Beckwith, Howard O. Sturges, C. W. Lippitt, George M. Smith, C. Mauran, Charles Adams, E. P. Mason, J. L. Moss, Jr., and Joseph Harris.

The Military and Veterans of the War formed on Broadway in the following order :

POLICE SKIRMISHERS.

Platoon of Police under Sergeant Warner.

Chief Marshal, Maj. Gen. A. E. Burnside, with the following Assistant Marshals: Gen. Lewis Richmond, Gen. C. H. Tompkins, Gen. James Shaw, Jr., Gen. John G. Hazard, Gen. Nathan Goff, Jr., Gen. Nelson Viall,

Gen. Horatio Rogers, Gen. Henry T. Sisson, Gen. William Ames, Gen. Charles R. Brayton, Gen. George W. Tew, Col. George H. Browne, Col. John T. Pitman, Col. Edwin Metcalf, Col. E. H. Rhodes, Col. Willard Sayles, Col. R. H. I. Goddard, Col. J. Albert Munroe, Col. S. B. M. Read.

THE VETERAN DIVISION.

GEN. CHARLES R. BRAYTON, commanding the Veterans of the Army and Navy, with the following aids: Col. E. H. Rhodes, A. A. G. and chief of staff; Major E. C. Pomroy, Assistant Quastermaster General; Col. William H. Walcott, Capt. John M. Barker, Major Edwin Stanley, Capt. John E. Burroughs, Capt. George W. Weeden, Major L. Travers, Capt. William B. Rhodes, Capt. D. H. Finley, Capt. James P. Rhodes, Maj. J. B. Greene, Maj. John E. Bradford, Col. Daniel R. Ballou, Capt. Israel R. Sheldon, Capt. James S. Hudson; W. B. Westcott, Assistant Inspector General; Col. Edwin Metcalf, Judge Advocate; James B. Buffum, Chaplain.

DEPARTMENT OFFICERS.

Capt. Ira H. Parkis, Sr. Vice Department Commander; Captain George T. Easterbrooks, Jr., Vice Department Commander.

COUNCIL ADMINISTRATION.

Sergeant Wm. Millen, Major George F. Crowninshield, Captain James Aborn, Captain Frank H. Wilkes, P. M. Barber, 2d.

AIDS.

Col, Wm. H. Walcott, Capt. John M. Barker, Major Edwin Stanley, Capt John E. Burroughs, Capt. George W. Weeden, Maj. L. Travers, Major Wm. D. C. Finley, Capt. James P. Rhodes, Major J. B. Greene, Major John E. Bradford, Col. Daniel R. Ballou, Capt. Israel R. Sheldon, Capt. James S. Hudson.

AMERICAN BRASS BAND.

D. W. Reeves, Leader. 30 Pieces.

POST NO. 1, PROVIDENCE.

Capt. Wm. Stone, Commander, Gilbert Wilson, Senior Vice Commander, Capt. Benj. C. Hall, Junior Vice Commander; Capt. C. Henry Barney, Adjutant; Capt. William Frankland, Quartermaster; Twelve Companies—370 men, Second Rhode Island, and California Colors.

Gen. William Cogswell, Department Commander, of Massachusetts, with Surgeon Green and Major Sears, of his staff, in Barouche.

NEWPORT BRASS BAND.

Nineteen Pieces.

POST NO. 2, NEWPORT.

Capt. Geo. C. Williams, Commander; Samuel Beaumont, Senior Vice Commander; Jas. W. Dennis, Junior Vice Commander; J. McCarty, Adjutant ; J. B. Mason, Quartermaster, our companies—80 men, Fourth Rhode Island Colors.

POST NO. 3 CENTRAL FALLS.

Maj. Henri Bacon, Commander; S. B. Binney, Senior Vice Commander; J. A. Jones, Junior Vice Commander; Maj. John Aigan, Adjutant; Major G. F. Crowninshield, Quartermaster, three companies—75 men, Seventh Rhode Island Colors.

POST NO. 4, BRISTOL.

Frank G. Bourne, Commander; A. A. Munroe, Senior Vice Commander; E. S. Congdon, Junior Vice Commander; J. T. Phillips, Adjutant; J. C. Witherton, Quartermaster; two companies—42 men, 2d R. I. Colors.

POST NO. 5, ASHAWAY.

P. M. Barber, Commander; B. D. Tenant, Senior Vice Commander; J. Bellany, Junior Vice Commander; E. G. Crandall, Adjutant; M. S. Rodman, Quartermaster; three companies—60 men, Third Rhode Island Heavy Artillery Colors.

THE FULL WHATCHEER BAND.

W. C. Sperry, Leader.

POST NO. 6, WESTERLY.

George Carmichael, Commander; two companies—40 men, Fifth Rhode Island Artillery Colors.

POST NO. 7, EAST GREENWICH.

G. S. Burton, Commander; R. C. Gardner, Senior Vice Commander; N. W. Taber, Junior Vice Commander; E. B. Taber, Adjutant; W. D. Gardner, Quartermaster; two companies—40 men, First R. I. Infantry Colors.

POST NO. 8, PHENIX.

C. P. Williams, Commander; F. W. Lark, Senior Vice Commander; W. Johnson, Junior Vice Commander; W. E. Sweet, Adjutant; R. H. Northup, Quartermaster; five companies—100 men, Fifth Rhode Island Heavy Artillery Colors. Disabled Veterans in ten barouches.

POST NO. 9, WOONSOCKET.

Major S. H. Brown, Commander; J. H. Richard, Sr. Vice Commander; G. A. Reed, Junior Vice Commander; J. A. Gardner, Adjutant; J. Pickford, Quartermaster, three companies—75 men, Third Rhode Island Artillery Colors.

BAND 5th U. S. ARTILLERY.

Ludwig Frank, Leader, Twenty-Five Pieces.

POST NO. 10, PROVIDENCE.

H. B. Barker, Commander; C. H. Williams, Senior Vice Commander;

A. H. Spencer, Junior Vice Commander; G. H. Pettis. Adjutant; W. Palmer, Quartermaster; twelve companies—250 men, Fifth and Seventh Rhode Island Infantry and Third Artillery Colors.

FALL RIVER CORNET BAND.

POSTS 11 AND 12 PROVIDENCE.

Col. R. H. I. Goddard, Commander; Captain Elisha Dyer, Senior Vice Commander; Capt. G. W. Darling, Junior Vice Commander; C. H. Chase, Adjutant; Lieut. Amos M. Bowen, Quartermaster; ten companies—200 men, with colors, 11th and 4th Rhode Island Infantry.

POST NO. 13, PROVIDENCE.

R. F. Nicola, Commander; L. G. Phenix, Senior Vice Commander; C. C. Johnson, Junior Vice Commander; G. N. Black, Adjutant; J. Howland, Quartermaster; two companies—40 men with colors, 10th and 25th Army Corps and 14th Rhode Island.

POST NO. 14, NATICK.

Peter Whalen, Commander; John Wells, Senior Vice Commander; John Devlin, Junior Vice Commander; J. A. C. Patterson, Adjutant; J. N. Downing, Quartermaster; two companies—40 men, 2d R. I. Infantry Colors.

POST NO. 15, SLATERSVILLE.

Nathan Benton, Commander; J. H. Parkis, Senior Vice Commander ; F. Colwell, Junior Vice Commander; A. A. Mowry, Adjutant; Isaac Place, Quartermaster; one company; Revolutionary Colors.

POST NO. 16, HOPE VALLEY.

L. W. A. Cole, Commander; H. R. Gates, Senior Vice Commander; G. N. Nichols, Junior Vice Commander; R. E. Gardner, Adjutant; F. M. Benton, Quartermaster ; one company—60 men, Post Colors.

THE MILITIA.

MAJOR GENERAL HORACE DANIELS, commanding Rhode Island Militia, with the following staff; Colonel Heber Le Favour, Chief of Staff; Major R. W. Burlingame, Quartermaster General; Major Ed. A. Greene, Paymaster General; Major Daniel S. Dexter, Commissary General; Major Thomas S. Perry, Surgeon General; Maj. H. A. Goodwin, A. D. C.

TAUNTON NATIONAL BAND,

E. D. Ingraham, Leader, Twenty-Four Pieces.

NEWPORT ARTILLERY.

In two sections, acting as body guard to His EXCELLENCY GOVERNOR PADELFORD. Col. John Hare Powell, Lieut, Col. A. P. Sherman, Maj. T, S. Burdick, Capt. Thomas Nason, Quartermaster George H. Vaughn, Paymaster, W. G. Stevens, Commissary G. A. Simmons, Surgeon N. G. Stanton, Assistant Surgeon J. H. Taylor; 100 men rank and file.

FIRST SECTION NEWPORT ARTILLERY.

Composed of two companies commanded as follows: First Company, Lt. Col. A. P. Sherman; 2d company, Capt. T. S. Nason, carriage containing HIS EXCELLENCY GOVERNOR PADELFORD, Adjutant Gen. E. C. Maurau, Commissary Gen. William Gilpin, and Col. W. A. Steadman.

GOVERNOR'S PERSONAL STAFF.

Mounted as follows: Col. B. F. Remington, Col. Christopher Rhodes, Col. Daniel T. Lyman, and Col. J. T. Murray.

GOVERNOR'S GENERAL STAFF.

Mounted as follows: Quartermaster General Lysander Flagg, Capt. Edwin A. Browne and Capt. George O. Willard of his staff, Paymaster Gen. J. C. Knight, Assistant Surgeon General A. G. Browning, Judge Advocate General John Turner, and Capt. D. A. Waldron, of Gen. Gilpin's staff.

SECOND SECTION NEWPORT ARTILLERY.

In two companies, commanded as follows: Third company, Quartermaster G. H. Vaughn; fourth company, Major T. S. Burdick.

FIRST BRIGADE.

Brigadier Gen. Arnold, L Burdick commanding, Staff Brigade Inspector C. L. Devins, Quartermaster, A. C. Landers; Aids, William W. Marvel.

REDWOOD BAND,

Of Newport. 24 Pieces, A. W. Haynes, Leader.

NEWPORT FIRST LIGHT INFANTRY ZOUAVES.

Col. G. W. Sherman; Lieut. Col. W. Cook Hazard; Capt. James Hogan, Adjutant, F. S. Hazard; Quartermaster, Thomas Chambers; Commissary S. D. Goff; Lieut., Otto Guidice; 75 men—rifles.

WARREN DRUM BAND.

Drum Major, W. A. Day; Ten Drums.

WARREN ARTILLERY.

Col. John Livesey; Lt. Col. Chas. D. Kelley; Major, J. White; Adjutant, J. Prior; Quartermaster, F. E. Dana; Surgeon, Gilbert Clarke; Paymaster, W. B. Crowell; Capt. J. Makepiece; Lieut., H. Birch; 40 men—rifles.

AQUIDNECK RIFLES,

Of Newport. Captain, William K. Delaney; 1st Lieutenant, Michael McCormick; 2d Lieut., Morris Horrigan; 51 men—muskets.

BRISTOL LIGHT INFANTRY.

Captain D. Fanning; 1st Lieutenant, Thomas Connelly; 2d Lieutenant, William Duffee; 61 men—muskets.

BURNSIDE GUARDS

Of Newport, Captain, Collins S. Burrell; 1st Lieut., James W. Johnson; 2d Lieut., J. P. Easton; 45 men (colored), muskets.

BRISTOL CORNET BAND.

A. B. Winch, Leader, 20 Pieces.

BRISTOL TRAIN OF ARTILLERY.

Col. James B. Burgess; Lt. Col. Edmund Horton; Maj. Alden Fish; Capt. John V. Lewis; Lieut. James Anderson; Quartermaster and Clerk, Frank L. Hoar; 50 men—rifles.

SECOND BRIGADE.

Brigadier General William R. Walker, with the following staff officers: Major S. R. Bucklin, Chief of Staff; Quartermaster, Capt. John W. Tillinghast; Paymaster, Capt. G. W. Newell; Commissary, Capt. T. C. LeValley; Surgeon, Stephen F. Fiske; Judge Ad., E. A. Perrin; Aid, Henry C. Pierce.

GILMORE'S BAND,

Of Pawtucket, W. E. Gilmore Leader, 30 Pieces.

First Battalion, Col. E. L. Freeman, commanding. Staff—Major, James M. Davis; Surgeon, A. A. Mann; Quartermaster, Geo. W. Barry; Quartermaster Sergt. C. F. Crawford.

UNION GUARDS, CENTRAL FALLS.

Captain Robert A. Robertson; Lieutenants David L. Sheldon; Benjamin W. Buffum—50 muskets.

PAWTUCKET LIGHT GUARDS.

Col. Robert McCloy; Lieut. Col. O. H. Perry; Major Geo. A. Mason; Staff—Adjutant, H. C. Brown; Quartermaster, J. A. Brown; Paymaster, James M. Crawford; Commissary, J. E. Dispeau; Surgeon, Freeman Berry, Jr.; Assistant Surgeon, J. J. Sherman; Capt. C. B. Hathaway; Lieutenants P. Tower, Henry Read. 48 muskets.

DRUM CORPS.

SMITHFIELD RIFLES.

Captain, P. D. Hall; Lieuts. H. E. Dines; William Winterbottom. 42 men. Five veteran soldiers accompanied the Rifles.

MILFORD BRASS BAND.

H. French, Leader, Eighteen Pieces.

2

WOONSOCKET GUARDS.

Col. J. R. Waterhouse; Lieut. Col. N. A. Vaslet: Major J. McClarron; Capt. E. E. Pearce; Lt. A. Young; Staff Adjutant, E. H. Dudley; Quartermaster E. Thurber; Paymaster, C. Darling; Surgeon, Godfrey Miller; 18 muskets.

SECOND BATTALION.

Captain, Charles R. Dennis, Commanding.

GILMORE'S BAND BOSTON.

M. Arbuckle, Leader, Thirty Pieces.

LIGHT INFANTRY DRUM CORPS.

Major R. W. Potter, Leader.

FIRST LIGHT INFANTRY.

Three companies, sixty-five muskets, Capt. Charles R. Dennis commanding; Lieut. E. B. Bullock commanding Company A., Lieut. J. J. Jenckes commanding Company B., Lieut. E. F. Annable commanding Company C.; Lieut. J. L. Sherman: Staff Quartermaster, F. J. Sheldon; Paymaster, W. H. Teel; Assistant Paymaster, H. L. Parsons; Commissary, H. J. Steere; Inspector, Col. W. W. Brown; Chaplain, Rev. S. H. Webb. Guests of the F. L. I. Officers of State Guard, Worcester, Mass.

INFANTRY CADETS.

Four companies, eighty-five muskets; Capt. E. W. Bucklin; Lieut. E. W. Allen, commanding Co. A.; Lieut. Arthur Brown, commanding Co. B.; Lieut. Frank Sheldon, Co. C.; Lieut. F. S. Arnold, Co. D.

SLOCUM LIGHT GUARD.

With the Brigade Colors, 28 muskets Major James Smith, commanding; Captain H. M. Howe, Lieut. E. M. Young.

THIRD BATTALION.

Col. Henry Allen, commanding.

BROWN'S BRIGADE BAND, Boston.

H. C. Brown, Leader. 30 pieces.

UNITED TRAIN OF ARTILLERY.

Two companies, with Color Guard, 74 muskets, Colonel Henry Allen; Lieutenant Colonel, Augustus Wright; Major, Wm. H. Mason; Capt. George A. Dodge; Staff-Adjutant, T. W. Chace; Quartermaster, E. A. Calder; Paymaster, B. F. Peabodie; Commissary, H. E. Metcalf; Assistant Quartermaster, E. H. Rockwell; Assistant, Orray Taft, Jr., Assistant Surgeon, H. C. Spencer. Guests of the United Train of Artillery,—Capt. L. D. Bulkley; Lieut. Benj. Gurney, Sergeant, John Martine; Private George H. Chatterton,—of the "Old Guard," New York.

FOURTH BATTALION.

Col. James Moran, Commanding.

NORTH ATTLEBORO' CORNET BAND.

H. E. Lincoln, Leader, 25 pieces.

DRUM CORPS.

RHODE ISLAND GUARDS.

Five companies. Col. James Moran; Adjutant, D. J. Mykins; Major, James Larkin; Captain, William H. Grimes; Sergeant, Major Thos. Keeffe. Co. A.—Capt. Edward Moran; Lieutenants, J. Robinson, J. H. McGaran—45 muskets. Co. B.—Captain, Bernard Flynn; Lieutenants, J. Cullen, Owen Goodwin,—40 muskets. Co. C.—Capt. J. J. Moriarty; Lieutenants, John McGraff, John Farrell. 40 muskets. Co. D.—Capt. John Rebens; Lieuts. J. E. Kearn, M. F. McCanna. 40 muskets. Co. F.—(formerly Lonsdale Infantry,) Capt. John Carrigan; Lieuts. James Slaine, Patrick Sullivan, 35 muskets.

KEARNEY DRUM CORPS.

KEARNEY CADETS.

Forty five muskets. Capt. M. F. Munnegle; Lieuts. A. P. Lynn, J. A. Johnson. Staff—Quartermaster, William Johnson; Paymaster, P. G. Fox; Commissary, James W. Nolan.

FIFTH BATTALION.

Major Zebedee Howland, Commanding.

DRUM CORPS.

BURNSIDE NATIONAL GUARDS.

Three companies. Col. Z. Howland; Adjutant, George H. Blair; Quartermaster, E. J. Morris; Surgeon, Jerome Morgan. Co. A.—Capt. J. A. Munroe; Lieuts. W. H. Scott, A. M. Lawrence. 45 muskets. Co. B—Captain L. G. Phenix; Lieuts. Alfred Smith, Thomas Brinn. 50 muskets. Co. C.—Capt. J. A. Creighton; Lieuts. L. Kennegee, Albro Lyons. 50 muskets.

FOURTH BRIGADE.

Brigadier General James Waterhouse, Commanding. Staff Officers—Major Jonathan M. Wheeler, Captain Israel R. Sheldon, Captain Albert C. Dedrick.

WOONSOCKET CORNET BAND.

B. W. Nichols, leader, 21 pieces.

WESTERLY RIFLES.

Two companies. 98 muskets. Lieut. Col. J. Clarke Barber, Adjutant H. Swan, Paymaster S. H. Peabody, Surgeon C. N. Lewis, Asst. Surgeon E. H. Knowles, Chaplain S. H. Cross. Co. C.—Capt. Daniel L. Champlin; Lieuts. Samuel Blevin, Alfred B. Dyer. Co. B.—Capt. J. C. Babcock; Lieutenants George C. Stillman, J. B. Brown.

KENTISH ARTILLERY,

Apponaug. 53 muskets. Col. Wm. H. Baker; Lieut. Col. Jason T.

Wood; Maj. George Blackmore; Capt. H. J. Wilbur; Staff—Adjutant Henry Matteson; Paymaster J. G. Browning; Quartermaster J. T. Potter; Commissary John Pettis; Past Lieut. Col. S. W. Clarke

DRUM CORPS.
KENTISH GUARDS.

East Greenwich. 58 muskets. Col. Lyman Himes, Lieut. Col. Warren D. Gardner, Major S. P. Lowell, Capt. Rowland Fish, Lt. Wm. Daven.

MYSTIC UNION BAND.

S. Gallup, leader, 19 pieces.

WEST GREENWICH CADETS.

Sixty muskets. Col. James P. Briggs, Lieut. Col. H. C. Shippee, Major J. A. Hall, Capt. Stephen Johnson, Lieutenants G. W. Fish, J. A. Shippee, Paymaster Pardon Hopkins.

WOLFE TONE GUARDS.

Forty-two muskets. Capt. J. Costine, Lieuts. William McPherson, J. Hickey; Adjutant, Garrett Walsh; Paymaster, J. J. Sullivan.

ARTILLERY BATTALION.

Major Edward G. Mead, commanding. Aids—Col. Elisha Dyer, Jr., and Major W. C. Simmons.

PROVIDENCE MARINE CORPS OF ARTILLERY.

Major G. R. Brown, Capt. W. E. Cushing, Lieut. Stephen Trippe, Lieut. J. M. Hull, Adjutant Robert Grosvenor, Commissary R. H. Deming, Paymaster E. M. Hunt, Orderly G. B. Burlingame. Full battery of six pieces, battery wagon and forge.

WOONSOCKET LIGHT ARTILLERY.

Capt. Henry J. White, 1st Lieut. Chas. M. Arnold, 2d. Lieut. Philo E. Thayer, 3rd Lieut. Elisha Colvin. Full battery of four pieces, 78 men.

TOWER LIGHT BATTERY.

Pawtucket. Lieut. W. W. Dexter, commanding, 1st Lieut. John Allen, 2d Lieut. Ansel Sweet. Full battery of four pieces, 65 men.

CAVALRY BATTALION.

Col. Frederick Miller, Commander.

PROVIDENCE HORSE GUARDS.

Lieut. Col. J. Lippitt Snow, commanding; Major Stephen Brownell, Adjutant C. F. Taylor, Paymaster C. A. Hubbard, Capt. A. O. Bourne, Capt. C. H. Sprague, Lieut. J. C. King. 50 men.

PAWTUCKET HORSE GUARDS.

Capt. H. J. Hall, 1st Lieut. H. H. Richardson, 2d Lieut. S. B. Lord. Honorary Staff—Capt. F. M. Bates, Capt. Obadiah Brown, Surgeon J. C Budlong, Chaplain S. L. Gracie. 55 men.

The line of march was through Broadway, Knight, High, Broad, Dorrance, Westminster, South Main, Transit, Benefit, Meeting, North Main, and Steeple Streets, to Exchange Place and the Monument. A perfect ovation greeted the column along the whole distance. Flags and decorations were in abundance, sidewalks, housetops, windows, and every conceivable place that would afford a view of the procession was occupied. Waving handkerchiefs were met at every step, and everything indicated that the dedicating services were a willing tribute from a grateful people. There were nearly two thousand Veterans in the ranks.

The procession reached Exchange Place about one o'clock, when the Newport Artillery, the Governor's Body-Guard, escorted him to the stand near the Monument. The companies of Veterans then formed in a solid body at the lower part of the open space with the Uniformed Militia in a compact form in the rear, the lines extending entirely across Exchange Place. When the word was given, this great body of men, more than four thousand in number, marched in division front up the wide thoroughfare towards the monument. The solid host, the many tattered battle flags, the blue uniforms of the Veteran Corps, the brilliant clothes of the citizen soldiers, the gleaming of the muskets and bayonets, and the firm and regular marching to the music of sixteen bands, was a sight never to be forgotten by those who witnessed it. As the column advanced, the spectators on the stand and the immense crowd which filled the side walks and grounds adjacent to the Monument and Railroad Depot, applauded, cheered and waved their handkerchiefs over and over again.

As soon as General Burnside, Chief Marshal, had massed the Veterans and the Military, he despatched one of his

Assistants to the Committee on the platform, to make it known, and took his stand with a large number of officers, including several from other States, upon the buttresses and steps of the Monument. The services now commenced and proceeded as follows:

Dedication Overture arranged for the occasion, by the American Brass Band.

Chorus, "God of Israel," by a Choir of three hundred singers, under the direction of Edwin Baker, Esq.

Introductory remarks by His Excellency Governor Padelford, as follows :

Fellow Citizens :—The occasion which has called us together this day is the most memorable that has ever occurred in our history. We meet to do honor to the brave men who have given up their lives for their country, and whose names, on tablets of bronze, are immortalized on the beautiful monument about to be uncovered before you. Like all the works of man, granite and bronze may in time crumble and decay; but the memory of these brave men will not perish. While time lasts, their sacrifices will form a brilliant page in the history of their country, shedding a bright lustre on their native State, forever covering them with imperishable glory and renown.

Let us be grateful to Divine Providence that so many who went forth to do battle, were permitted to return, and are present with us on this occasion. Their hearts must be moved with a feeling of just pride, that the memory of their comrades in arms is this day to be consecrated, not only by monumental art, but by suitable exercises before this vast assemblage of our fellow citizens from all parts of our beloved State.

It is a fitting occasion for us all to drink at the fountains of Divine inspiration, lessons of wisdom and of patriotism for our future guidance in life.

It is not becoming for me to speak at this time of the daring deeds of our soldiers, or of the grand results to humanity and to the world, which the war has effected. This will be done by one who has alike stood by them in battle, and who has administered spiritual comfort to them in the hour of death.

Let the Monument be uncovered !

While the curtain which enveloped the Monument was being slowly withdrawn, a dirge was played by the Band.

The solemnity of the spectacle touched the hearts of the spectators and drew tears from hundreds. But when the whole structure appeared with its beautiful bronze statues, cheer upon cheer, loud and long, arose from the vast multitude which filled the square. Mr. Rogers, the sculptor and designer of the Monument, being called for, came forward and was presented to the spectators by the Hon. William Grosvenor, one of the State Committee, and loudly cheered. The State Committee, under whose charge the Monument had been executed, were next called for, when they appeared, made their acknowledgment, and were also cheered.

Prayer was offered by the Rev. Dr. Thayer, of Newport.

Chorus, "The Lord is Great," was sung by the Choir.

The Rev. Augustus Woodbury was then introduced and delivered the Oration.

THE ORATION.

FELLOW - CITIZENS, COMRADES, FRIENDS : There seems scarcely a place for words in the presence of this memorial of immortal deeds. The structure,—the occasion,—speaks. Those mute figures which represent the defenders of the Republic by land and sea, are vocal above the power of human speech. That long list of brave men who passed through seas of blood, and at last died that the nation might live, is at once the eulogy and the perpetual record of a virtue, which survives death. This vast concourse, gathered from every part of our State, attests the desire of the people to honor the memory of those who fell in their defence. This assembly of comrades, of the same grand army of the living and the dead, speaks of victory won through severest struggles, and peace secured through sanguinary strife. Those tattered flags, rent by the missiles of the foe, and begrimmed by the dust and smoke of battle, add their pathetic story of heroism and sacrifice. The day itself recalls the memories of that great conflict in which our best and bravest fell. How little can be expressed by words that reach only the bodily ear, while these voices are speaking to the soul! At best, it can be but a feeble offering that I bring to the departed, and a simple flower that I cast upon their graves.

3

The erection of this monument has a profoundly important purpose. It is to perpetuate the remembrance of what the men of Rhode Island did and suffered in behalf of the entire country. It is to aid in quickening the sentiment of patriotism in the national heart, and in educating the national character to a complete self-devotion to duty. When visiting Westminster Abbey, and contemplating the monuments of the worthies of English history, with which it is filled, I could not avoid the thought, that these were the teachers of a nation's life, as well as the witnesses to a nation's gratitude. For here the men, women and children of England could come to learn how "the path of duty" becomes "the way to glory." Here would be aroused the desire to emulate the greatness of which the marble told. We, indeed, have no Westminster Abbey, no venerable temple, beneath whose sacred roof a nation's pious and grateful care collects the ashes of her honored dead. But on every village green arises the "Soldiers' Monument," with its tale of a fidelity and courage, which shrank not from every danger, duty, hardship, sacrifice and death. Our memorial edifice is the vast temple built by the Almighty's hand, and domed by the over-arching sky. Here we raise the commemorative shaft, but more enduring still is the memory of the dead, enshrined, not in "storied urn," but in every loyal breast. I recall the famous words of Pericles in the funeral oration, which he pronounced in the early part of the Peloponnesian war, over the fallen Athenian youth : "Bestowing thus their lives upon the public, they have every one acquired a praise that will never decay, a sepulchre that will always be most illustrious—not that in which their bones lie mouldering, but that in which their fame is preserved, to be on every occasion eternally re-

membered, when honor is the employ of either word or
act. This whole earth is the sepulchre of illustrious men ;
nor is it the inscription on the columns in their native soil
alone that shows their merit, but the memorial of them,
better than all inscription, in every foreign nation, reposited
more durably in universal remembrance than on their own
tomb.''

These memorable names now thus inscribed belong to men
of every rank. There is no preëminence in death except
when value and virtue give it renown. The name of the private soldier has a place as lasting, as that of the general of
division which heads the roll. Each one who did his work
and met his fate, as a brave man should, in the position to
which Providence assigned him, equally deserves an honora-
able commemoration. Some fell in battle on the land,
some found death upon the sea. The first and last struggle
of the war demanded each its victim. The life-blood of
some was the price of victory. The death of some added
to the anguish of defeat. Some died in the hospital,
some amid the horrors of the prison, and some were
privileged to breathe their last, soothed by the care of
friends and kindred. Some were laid away tenderly in the
soft bosom of the earth by loving hands, and some sleep in
unknown graves. All endured the toil, and fell by the
stroke of battle or disease, as Providence ordained. We
would here make no distinction. We judge of deeds, not
by the position, but by the personal character of him who
performs them, and by their own inherent worth. If the
quality of work be good, the place of performance is of
little account. Honor belongs to true manhood rather than
high rank, and lies in the spirit and manner of the doing
more than in the deed.

Another fact is here to be observed. Among the American soldiers and sailors were men of all degrees of privilege and training. The rich and the poor ; men who were tenderly nurtured and those who were taught in adversity's hard school ; the highly cultured and those of little learning ; men of mark and men of quiet life—of conspicuous fame and of an obscure career ; men of all creeds, of all parties, of all occupations, trades and professions ; of various nativity and different race—all these met and mingled, fused together in the fire of a common patriotism. Remember, that this was not a compulsory, but rather a voluntary service. Remember, that these men were accustomed, for the most part, to the comforts of well-ordered homes and peaceful avocations. Yet they freely undertook the performance of the most difficult tasks ; endured the hardships of the march, the voyage, the camp ; faced the dangers of battle on field and flood, with a calm courage or a daring bravery, which commanded the admiration of the veterans of disciplined armies and fleets. These men, in short, adjusted themselves to all the vicissitudes and exigencies of the war with a marvellous facility and flexibility of mind. This power of adaptation was as marked in the men of the regular, as in those of the volunteer service. Officers, whose duties had never exceeded the command of a seaside fort or frontier post, of an exploring party, or a single ship's crew, suddenly found themselves weighted with heavy responsibilities, and entrusted with enterprises of wide importance. Rising by quick promotion, they soon became charged with the leadership of large armies and fleets, and the conduct of a great war, in which the combatants were counted by the hundred thousand. Yet these men, of necessarily small experience, proved themselves equal to the nation's greatest demands. I speak, of course, in general terms. There was a certain proportion of cowardice, unfaithfulness, incompetence. But this proportion was never large, and when known, was condemned and quietly put aside.

Whence came this remarkable power of adaptation to the needs and duties of a great war? How did it happen to belong to men whose lives had mostly been spent in peace, and far away from any sound of arms—many of whom had to learn even the details of the manual from the start? Was it, that the American people were gifted with any special aptitude for a military life? Was there anything in our common modes of living that indicated the existence of any such capacity as was here displayed? Mr. Grote, the learned historian of Greece says: "Neither in the life of an individual, nor in that of a people, does the ordinary and every-day movement appear at all worthy of those particular seasons, in which a man is lifted above his own level, and becomes capable of extreme devotion and heroism. Yet such emotions, though their complete predominance is never more than transitory, have their foundations in veins of sentiment, which are not, even at other times, wholly extinct, but count among the manifold forces tending to modify and improve, if they cannot control human nature." It may have been so in our national life. Doubtless, on the surface, there was very little evidence of the great things beneath. Yet the patient and heroic qualities of manhood which the war demanded and developed, and which lifted the nation above its own level, were by no means accidental in their origin or sudden in their growth. They came up from a living root, which ran deep into the soil of the national character. The American citizen has had the

schooling of two centuries and a half of conflict with the
wilderness, with wild beasts, with savage men and savage
principles. Thus has he been trained to a quick adjustment
to new circumstances and strange conditions; to the necessity of preserving his own personal freedom and life,
and the public order; to the equal necessity of placing the
growing commonwealth beyond the reach of danger.
"Patriotism is impossible in a republic," said they who
did not appreciate the value of this life-long education.
"Our republic," we say in reply—and the word comes from
lips now silent in the dust; I read it between the lines of
yonder inscription—"Our republic is the great school of
patriotism." The American citizen accepts it as a part of
his religion, that the duty he owes to the State is next to
that he owes to his God! This sentiment, born within him,
grew with his growth, and became the dominant power
of his manhood's life.

At the basis of the American character there were certain principles, which, slowly developing amid the circumstances of American history, only awaited their occasion—
the principle of obedience to the constitutional pact; a
regard for law enacted by the representatives of the people;
submission of private advantage to public authority; sub-
ordination of personal interest to the public good; reverence
for the sacredness of self-government; and above all, and
beneath all, a deep conviction, that the body politic, which
grew out of the Declaration of Independence, was not a
mere confederacy of communities bound together by local
interest, but a nation, entitled to the service of all her
citizens to maintain her existence and heighten her glory—
a State, whose base was the fundamental law of a written
constitution, whose strength was in the loyalty of the

people, whose bonds of union were the obligations of patriotism, and whose increasing welfare was the prime object of political life! Forty years ago Jackson said : " The Constitution of the United States forms a government, not a league. Each state, having expressly parted with so many powers, as to constitute jointly with other states a single nation, cannot, from that period, possess any right to secede, because such secession does not break a league, but destroys the unity of a nation." The rebellion of the Southern States and the confederacy which they formed, violated all these principles, and so the loyal people of the Republic fought down the one, and destroyed the other.

Other elements were not wanting,—the perception of an ideal republic to be made real in this western world ; the knowledge of an imperative moral law to which states must bow ; faith in the power of religious truth, as prominent in the rudenesses of the pioneer's and the soldier's life, as in the refinements of settled and peaceful communities. The moral and ideal qualities of character, which have been the real substance of our national life from the first, cannot be left out of our estimate of the strength of the American Union. The power of the ideal is always the puzzle of human selfishness. When the South tried to break away from the North, it seemed, to all outward appearance, as though a general disintegration would take place. Our enemies abroad considered it as a foregone conclusion. Disloyal people at home talked of the impossibility of restoring the Union. Some among ourselves, at times, distrusted our own power. It was because the tenacity and durability of the ideal element of national life were not well understood. There was a certain allegiance to conscience, and a certain faith in truth, justice, righteousness and God,

which had underlain all our history and proved the salt of
all our life. That power which, step by step, and in the face
of dangers, difficulties and distresses, has reclaimed the
wilderness, and made it the abode of civilization and freedom,
has descended to us by direct inheritance. It came with our
fathers across the stormy seas ; it went with them through
the perils of our colonial history and the terrible struggle of
the Revolution ; it has gone with each successive stage in
our national progress to subdue the continent—the ideal,
moral, religious power, which dwelt in the hearts of the
people and gave them life ; taught them how to bear
adversity cheerfully ; saved them from the enervating influence of prosperous fortunes ; finally welded them together,
and made them capable of high and heroic deeds.

In no contest have ideas fought more conspicuously to
those who could see, than in this. On the one side were
liberty, human rights, civilization, the consecration of a continent to constitutional freedom. On the other side were
slavery, human wrongs, the barbarism which is always in-
separable from an irresponsible despotism, the dominion of a
continent in the interests of oppression. The stronger and
better ideas triumphed, as they always will and always must.
In the nature of things, there could be but one result—the
reëstablishment of the State and its enthronement on a
position alike impregnable to foreign and domestic foes.
That which conquered was not altogether the power of
superior numbers, but rather the power of superior ideas.
Behind that was faith in those ideas and in God, firmly
abiding in the popular heart, expressed in the remarkable
state papers of the Executive, deeply fixed and faithfully
cherished, amid all temporary discouragements and sometimes
disheartening defeats. This carried us through the conflict

to its victorious end. It destroyed slavery, secession and treason. It made the Union secure. It commanded, as well for the finally successful cause as for the emancipation of the slaves, "the considerate judgment of mankind, and the gracious favor of Almighty God."

It is not often that a great cause has for its foundation, and for the impulse of its promotion, such depth and power of moral earnestness. It is not surprising that, in an age given over to the pursuit of material ends, the moral power of the loyal states should have been underrated and their purpose misunderstood, both at home and abroad. It was no struggle for empire between rival factions or rival sections, as some foreigners professed to believe. It was the heart of the nation striving to live and perpetuate its life. Those, who sought to destroy the Union, did not know the strength of the sentiment they were trying to uproot. We, who sought to preserve the Republic, held back with long forbearance from the war for which the South was urgent. We hoped that the strife unto blood might be averted. We remembered how closely the North and South had stood together in the past, in defence of the commonwealth. We could hardly believe that an American hand would willingly strike the separating blow, which would deprive us of our common heritage and our common hope. So, when the war came, we accepted its prosecution as a duty to be performed with persistence, but not with bitterness or hatred. When the war ended, we applied ourselves at once to the work of binding up the wounds, and closing the breaches it had made. We demanded, that its results should be accepted by those who provoked it. We still demand it. But, severe as the contest was, I doubt if there remains, in the hearts of those who conquered, any feeling of personal animosity

4

toward those who failed. When the strife was over all such hostility was buried out of sight. God grant that for it there may be no resurrection!

The moral earnestness which entered into the conflict deepened the sense of personal responsibility. The loyal citizen, educated to a love of free institutions, saw a personal danger in the peril that threatened them. He had come to feel that in them individual freedom had its best guaranty. The free state protects, and is protected by the free man. Each draws life from the other. Neither can exist apart. The preservation of the Republic is the preservation of the citizen. There is no ideal excellence, of which the citizen dreams, that may not belong to the State, of which he is a part. By this intimate interweaving of needs, interests, duties, ambitions, is produced that texture of national life, which is too tenacious to be rent asunder by violence, and too enduring to be worn away by time. American institutions have their assurance of stability in the power of individual patriotism. Each citizen can say: "I am the State." Each citizen will swear: "While I live, the State shall have a defence and support."

In the camp, and under the despotism of martial law, the soldier was still a citizen. He had his own opinions in regard to questions of public policy, and could judge intelligently of the plans discussed in the cabinet, and the movements executed in the field. He voted. He had his daily mail and his daily newspaper. He was in constant communication with his home, and knew precisely what was uppermost in the public mind. His military life lay upon the broad basis of his intelligent political duty. Martinets, who wished to make the army a machine, old soldiers who were accustomed to the routine of military discipline, shook their heads, doubted, complained, possibly feared, that this sense of citizenship would spoil the soldier. But the army that saved the Repu'lic was never a machine, but rather a living organism, that moved and acted from the impulse of its own innate vital force. In actual warfare, the most thoughtful and intelligent soldier was the most trustworthy—the best, foremost, and most steadfast. It seemed difficult for those who stood on an equal footing at home, to recognize and observe the distinctions of rank in the field. But here the good sense of the American character prevented any disturbance of order. Breaches of discipline occurred among the unthinking and reckless, who are always reluctant to submit to authority. But, in general, the citizen soldier easily fell into the place in which his particular duty was to be performed. For the time he held in abeyance his democratic prerogatives, and accepted the situation, as it was then proposed to him. He sacrificed his personal independence to his duty to the imperilled State.

Thus it happened that the armies in the field were always loyal, both to their immediate commanders and to the general government. The attachments formed in army life are proverbially strong. A popular commander—as with hooks of steel—binds the hearts of his soldiers closely to himself. It is no slight matter to remove from command a chief, to whom service has become like personal devotion. When the government found it necessary to perform this ungracious duty, the soldiers readily acquiesced, and bated not a title of their obedience to the new leader. The Army of the Potomac had, from first to last, no less than five different commanders. In the chief command of our western armies frequent changes took place. Yet the allegiance of our citizen soldiers was unchanged, though their affections were sometimes sorely tried. Whatever may be said or thought of others, they always stood firm to their duty. In their clear perception of duty they assured themselves that in the business of war, the prime obligation was hearty, unquestioning obedience to a superior in rank. When it is remembered —as it always should be remembered—that these were not veterans, accustomed by long service to obey, and knowing no other rule, but citizens, who were wonted to independent thought and action, and had lately been transplanted from the freedom of home-life to the restraints of the camp, the phenomenon was truly wonderful. Germany, in the recent war, has shown something similar, though not altogether like. For her landwehr and landsturm constitute a vast military organization, with stated and regular terms of service. In no nation of modern times, I can safely say, has such an army of citizen soldiers, with such facility, been raised, organized, trained to war ; taught to turn the hand from plough, anvil, hammer, plane, pen, pencil, book to musket, bayonet, cannon, cutlass, sword, and found equally efficient in the use of either implement. It is to the exceeding honor of the American citizen that he could thus easily assume these new duties, and submit himself to this new control.

In speaking thus warmly of our volunteer forces, I would, in no way, disparage the services of the regular and navy. Especially would I recognize the importance of a military and naval education. The country cannot dispense with its national schools at West Point and Annapolis. We must always have, as we shall always need, well-trained officers to organize, to plan, to direct. But after all, the nation's chief reliance must be, not upon large standing armies and fleets, but upon her own citizens, loyal, facile, intelligent, patriotic, always ready for a self-forgetful, devoted service. It was gratifying to perceive the general spirit of cordialty with which the regular and volunteer officers, both in army and navy, fraternized with one another. There could be no rivalry, except in striving to prove who could serve the best and sacrifice the most. Side by side on yonder tablet are the names of Stevens and Rodman—friends, comrades, brothers in arms, officers in the same corps—fit representatives of the regular and volunteer service. The one was educated at the national military academy. The other came from business life. Is the laurel of the one greener than that of the other? Is the memory of the one dearer than that of the other? Equally brave, equally devoted, no jealousy disturbed their friendship in life, or obscured their glory in death. The chief question between such men as these, both then and now, is, what service can each best render to the common mother of them all?

It was also pleasing to observe the confidence which was reposed in our volunteer officers and soldiers by the best generals in the regular army. Grant gave to Butler, and—no wise discouraged by his failure—to Terry, the opportunity of capturing Fort Fisher, and of winning the honor of that brilliant exploit. The most effective operation of the war—Sherman's march to the sea—was successfully performed by a force composed almost entirely of a volunteer soldiery. For Sherman knew the men he trusted, and trusted them without reserve. So Farragut, with unrivalled bravery and skill, opened the way for the volunteer soldier to occupy New Orleans and Mobile. So Foote, with scarcely less gallantry, cleared our western rivers for the victorious progress of our arms by land. The faithful servants of the Republic seek only to serve her well. The trained soldier and sailor, the citizen and volunteer, unite in patriotic duty. The country remembers both with equal gratitude, and gives to both, as now and here, an equal and imperishable honor.

There was a certain poetic and religious element which wound its silver thread through the dark texture of the strife, to enliven and beautify it. It was noticed, both in the active duty of the march and even of the battle, and in the endurance of the hospital, that our soldiers had a great love for flowers, and in many instances a deep religious sentiment. After the battle of the Wilderness, was found upon the border of the field the body of a drummer boy, shot through and through. His hand clasped a bunch of violets, which he had plucked after he was struck, and on his face still lingered a smile of delight, as if the sweet familiar fragrance had overcome the pain of dying. Touching picture—but one of many! Almost every knapsack had a place for a copy of the New Testament, with a few dried leaves or flowers pressed within it, bits of poetry, and photographs of friends at home. The rose-bud brightened the dark uniform. The frequent song lightened the toil of the dusty road. In the hospital, what patience, what true and trusting faith soothed the long hours of pain and watching, or prepared the soul to meet the summons of death! The American soldier had a home behind him, and the sweet influence of that home sent a gleam of glory athwart the gloom of war. Love, hope and religion, that had made home beautiful for remembrance, still followed the young soldier. The father's honest pride, the mother's warm affection, the wife's earnest prayer, the fair maiden's love and longing—all came to mind and memory, as he stood in the front of the battle, or lay on his cot of suffering, and, while his heart softened into tenderness, it strengthened into heroism. He did the duty and bore the

pain the better, because of this blessed recollection and this
upward looking faith. As he died, beautiful visions of green
fields and spreading trees and glorious mountain-peaks, the
broad prairie, the waving grain, the village home, passed
before him. Soft eyes looked into his own from out the
gathering darkness, and gentle voices whispered to his
heart. No roar of cannon now, no clash of steel, but only
the prayers he had learned at his mother's knee, and the
memories of tender vows! Was it hard thus to die? The
brave youth only regretted, that he had but one life to give
to his country.*

In judging of the character of our patriotism, we must not
forget the influence of this home-life, to which I have just
alluded, nor must we pass over in silence the great part
which woman acted in the war. To the lessons of obedience and faithfulness she had taught in earlier years, to the
actual labor she performed at home and in the hospital, to
the enthusiasm and earnest interest she inspired, to the
prayers she uttered, to the saintly trust, the sublime patience she exhibited—even unconsciously to herself—we
are indebted more than we know. Without the woman's
help, man could have done but little. Without the spirit of
the woman's bravery, man could have fought his battles with
but slight success. There were invisible reënforcements
always marching to the field. There were supplies or courage and faith always going forward. The homes of the people were never exhausted, and out of them flowed the never-
failing streams which refreshed the nation's life. I remember now the earnest word of a poor, honest, humble wo-

---

*Nathan Hale, an American officer in the Revolution, was taken by the
British and executed, at New York, as a spy, Sept. 22, 1776. His last words
were: "I only regret that I have but one life to lose for my country."

man, which may well illustrate the spirit of our loyal home-life. She lived in some little country town in Massachusetts, and had come down to the hospital at Portsmouth Grove to see her son, who had been treated there, and was about re-turning to the army in the field. I happened to witness their parting as she went on board the boat that was to bring her up to the city. He was a bright, manly-looking youth —a private soldier. She kissed him, took his hand in hers, and said, "John, good bye, I may never see you again; but mind this, John, be sure and do your duty straight up to the handle!" "I will, mother," said he, in a cheery, yet somewhat tearful way—and so they separated. There was no doubt that he would! In talking with her while coming up the bay, I found that she belonged to that sturdy yeoman class of our people, from among whom the majority of our rank and file had been recruited—a thoroughly loyal American woman, who was willing to sacrifice much, and to endure much poverty and hard labor, if necessary. Three of her sons were already in the army, and the strain upon her was somewhat hard. But her brave heart never gave up, as though her own happiness and life were of little value in the time of the nation's necessity. It is a good illustration of the force that was in reserve, constantly sending forward its supports. The poor woman's phrase might have been more elegantly rendered, but the spirit and sentiment were there. Were they not everywhere, pervading the hearts of all our loyal women? I believe that the force, which these supplied, contributed very largely to the national success. Out of such sweet and tender life came forth an invincible strength!

The war came to an end, and the citizen soldiers of the Republic were to return to peaceful pursuits. Many anxious minds, not fully appreciating the capabilities of the American character, inquired whether these men had not been unfitted, by their military experience, for the occupations of civil life. The result proved the groundlessness of any fear or doubt of this kind. As the manner in which the people met the emergencies of the war was exceptional, so was the return of the soldiers to their social duties quite beyond the ordinary course. Silently and swiftly were they merged, with but few exceptions, into the great mass of our population. The public order felt no shock, the social state no disturbance. Those who had been conspicuous in the public eye, acting the great drama, of which all the world was a spectator, were content to retire to the obscurity of private life. No interests suffered. No rights were violated. On the contrary, the public welfare was promoted by the increase of productive labor. The country, already recovering from the blow she had received, has started forward on a course of prosperity, the end of which is beyond all our dreams of greatness. These men, instead of being demoralized by the war, seemed to have been touched by the spirit of a new consecration, as though the awful face of Duty had been unveiled before them, and their souls had been thrilled by her never-to-be-forgotten voice.

To deepen and strengthen the character—that was the result. And with such added strength and depth, the community could gratefully receive into its bosom the returning brave. As they marched back with firm step and bronzed faces, in clothing worn and defaced, bearing high the old flag, whose rags were more glorious than gilded banners, and whose faded inscriptions told of bloody fields, we welcomed them with a joy which was sometimes too deep for words. We looked along their ranks, and saw the vacant places which the storm of battle had made. Our eyes were wet with tears that came unbidden. Our heads were bowed in submission to that will which had ordered the event. In our hearts we made the vow that they who had fallen should never lack an honorable memorial; that their wounded and disabled comrades should never ask for sympathy and aid in vain; that their widows and orphans should never know want; that the cause for which they died should never be deserted or betrayed; and that we ourselves, taking new courage and faith from their example, would make the land we loved more worthy of so loyal a service and so costly a sacrifice. That vow is registered in Heaven and on the nation's heart, and by God's help it shall be faithfully kept.

While paying our honor to the dead, we would not forget the living veterans, who have "no cause to blush that they survive the battle." The nation owes its life to the exertions of these men—both the wounded and unscathed—and cannot well discharge the debt. So, to-day, I would plead in their behalf—not for alms, not for the charity that deprives one of self-respect, not for the gifts which are bestowed upon the disabled man, who wails forth his melancholy music from the curbstone of the street, but—for public employment, that they may, in the spirit of independent citizens, serve the country in peace as they did in war. So I urge, that whenever the country has any work to perform, which they are capable of doing, or any office of honor or emolument which they are fitted to fill, their claims should be remembered first of all. The Republic has not been wholly ungrateful in the past to those who have imperilled life and limb for her sake. The future shall show, that the American people have good memory for all faithful and patriotic deeds.

What now has come from all this ?   What has the country purchased with all these labors, strifes, sacrifices and griefs? Out of the terrible contest emerge two great ideas—Nationality and Free Citizenship. We are a compacted, united nation, a body politic, vital in every part. No one state has the headship. All are equal. Each is autonomous. But all are joined by an irrefragable bond of union. The Declaration of Independence now reaches its logical conclusion. The Constitution now receives its right interpretation.   Its magnificent preamble—pregnant with the life of centuries— we can now read, without hesitation and without reserve : "We, the people of these United States, in order to form a more perfect union, establish justice, insure domestic tranquility, provide for the common defence, promote the general welfare, and secure the blessings of liberty to ourselves and our posterity, do ordain and establish this Constitution of the UNITED STATES OF AMERICA." We now can comprehend what it is to be a nation and a power in the earth. The hope of the fathers is nearing its fruition. Their promise and prophecy to mankind is having its fulfilment.

One result, as encouraging to national virtue, as it is gratifying to national pride, is the position our success has given us among the nations of the world. The Union is now in no danger of being misunderstood. Success clears the eye of many a film, the mind of many a prejudice. If, as Jefferson said, the cause of the struggling colonies for independence was the cause of human nature, we can well say now, that the preservation of the Republic is a gain to human civilization everywhere. In the time of our extremity, foreign powers mistrusted our ability. In the time of our success they are eager to profess their confidence. No more significant act has been performed within the present century, than

the recent negotiation with Great Britain of the treaty of
Washington.   It is, as has been well said, "a new depart-
ure for mankind in the science of international law" and the
policy of international intercourse.   The United States and
England have laid the world under obligations of gratitude,
as they have shown, that two great nations with—as some
have thought—abundant reasons for war, can find still more
abundant reasons for peace, and can submit disputed questions of the highest importance to the tribunal of impartial
arbitration.   While others have wasted their strength by vin-
dictive war, clutching at each other's throat to gratify long-
cherished enmity, and laying up large stores for a future of
bitterest revenge, these two have gained the unwonted glory of proving, that national honor can consist with international amity.   Fortunate opportunity for us to be thus in-
strumental in promoting the welfare of humanity, and to
preach this new gospel of peace in the good old mother-
tongue !   But the opportunity came from our success.

It is not simply as a nation, but it is as a nation of free
men, that we stand in our place to-day.   How short a time
ago it was that the institution of slavery, cruel, aggressive,
defiant, ruled the land !   So powerful it seemed, that good
men mourned and wise men feared, when they contemplated
the future of the Republic.   It was so strong in its foundations, so well-supported, so fully fortified in public opinion,
so confident in itself, that the most clear-sighted could scarcely discern a ray of hope for its extinction.   The most san-
guine of its opponents only ventured to believe, that its fur-
ther extension could be stayed.   But Divine Providence had
decreed better things for us.   In the fire of the war the
chains of the bondman were melted.   Baptized with blood,
the slave arose from his degradation a free citizen of the Re-

public. It would have staggered credulity to be told, that a
result like that could be accomplished in half a century.
Behold, it required scarcely two years of strife to speak the
word of emancipation, but four years to make the word a
fact, and less than a decade to fix it forever in the fundamental national law! We fought the battle better than we
knew. The irresistible logic of events solved the problem.
Led by a power higher than ourselves, we marched on to
victories greater than we dreamed. Our eyes were blessed
with the vision of a glory which others had long desired to
see, but died without the sight. A grand imperial Union
arose with its zeal of free citizenship—without distinction
race, color, or previous condition of servitude—and took its
place unchallenged among the foremost powers of time. The
war gave us the opportunity of proving that a free citizen
is his country's best defender. Let peace enable us to prove,
that freedom of citizenship is the best element of a country's
enduring greatness. Let the nations be taught that the
American system of government—"of the people, by the
people, for the people"—is the most equitable among men;
that that empire is the best and the greatest, which has liberty for the corner-stone of its foundations, and equal justice between man and man, for the binding cement of its walls.
What mighty results hath God wrought through the instrumen-
tality of these humble, faithful men and women! We have
come to our triumph through great tribulation. But what a
triumph it is, and what transcendent possibilities for mankind are within it!

It is a grateful thought, to-day, that in these events, important to ourselves and to the interests of civilization everywhere the State of Rhode Island has borne a conspicuous
part. Her troops were among the earliest in the field and

among the last to leave it, having won a name for good discipline, for bravery, for endurance, for steady faithfulness in all positions, second to none. We would also gratefully recall the honorable services of those Rhode Island men, of different rank,—officers, soldiers, sailors—in the regiments of other states, in the regular army, navy and marine corps, whose gallantry and self devotion reflected glory on their state. All along the line, from the time that Burnside led the First Rhode Island to Washington, and Ives offered himself and his yacht to the government, to the firing of the last gun of the war, the men of Rhode Island made an illustrious record for us and for themselves. They served with Burnside, at Roanoke, Newbern, Fort Macon, South Mountain, and Knoxville; with Sherman, Hunter, Mitchell, and Gilmore at Port Royal, Pulaski, James Island and the siege of Charleston; with Butler and Banks at New Orleans; with McClellan at Yorktown, before Richmond and at Antietam; with Meade at Gettysburg; with Thomas at Nashville; with Sheridan in the Shenandoah Valley; with Grant at Vicksburg and in the long Virginia campaigns of 1864-65, which closed the war. Manassas, the Peninsula, Chantilly, Fredericksburg and Chancellorsville witnessed their unavailing valor. Their blood mingled with the waters of the Gulf of Mexico. The murderous fires of the Mississippi Passes lighted their path to victory under Farragut. The daring assault of Fort Fisher added to their renown. Goldsborough in Pamlico and Albermarle Sounds; Dupont at Hilton Head, and Dahlgren in Charleston harbor, saw and commended their bravery. What McDowell said on the eve of the first battle of Bull Run: "I rely on the Rhode Island brigade," has been confirmed upon a hundred fields. The State which gave a Greene and a Hopkins to the Revolution, and a Perry to the war of 1812, has not forgotten her ancient renown, and now stands among her sisters, wearing the bays which her sons have placed upon her brow. The principles which were the inspiration of her early life, have been the strength of her latter days. It is with a just and reasonable pride, that every citizen, from the humblest to the highest, can read the story, and feel that he can rightly share her fame. The people of our State, always remembering that they were Americans as well as Rhode Islanders, have given, indeed, a happy illustration of the truth, that Republican institutions, administered by an intelligent and virtuous democracy, can develope a patriotism, glorious in character, splendid in achievement, such as the world has rarely seen. No community has been more jealous of individual liberty and the rights of the State. No community has been more united in support of every measure adopted for the common defence. No community has given better and brighter evidence of devotion to the common good. The experience through which we passed, was sad, but we have been chastened for our profit. The test was searching, but we triumphantly sustained it. Now we are convinced, that what we have secured is worth all that it has cost. The Union stands, and it stands for liberty !

So we feel that these men have not died in vain. As those who have passed through the conflict, would refuse to yield a particle of that dear bought experience, so they who "bowed their noble souls to death," forbid us to believe that they have suffered thus for naught. Could a voice come down from those serene heights where souls of heroes dwell, it would have no doubtful tone, it would speak no hesitating word. "We are content," it would say : "To have died for liberty, to have saved the Republic, by our blood, to have put our lives in the breach, and thus to have closed the broken wall, that it might stand forever—this has been our privilege. We have given you a country which you will ever be proud to call your own. We have established in the western world an empire where a true freedom may abide in undisturbed possession, and peace may reign for the lasting welfare of mankind. We are content. It is for you to maintain inviolate the liberties we have won—to preserve the nation we have saved.',

"Yes, spirits of the heroic dead," we answer, "we here renew our vows. Here we consecrate ourselves afresh to the sustenance of the institutions, which your blood has sealed. Here we solemnly swear to keep unimpaired the inheritance you have bequeathed to us. By all your tears and toils, your pains and deaths, your contests and your triumphs, we pledge ourselves to an equal fidelity and an equal self-devotion. The way you have trod shall not be strange to our feet. The sufferings you have endured shall not affright our hearts. Whenever our dear mother shall call her sons to serve her, we will hear your voice, honored and glorified countrymen, cheering us on in the way of duty. Beneath its impulse and influence no path will be too difficult, no task too severe. How can we ever forget, how can we ever fail to imitate, your constancy and valor !"

FRIENDS : Is there not in all this an exceeding comfort to the heart bereaved ? The providential law demands sacrifice as the condition of the accomplishment of human good. Human lives must be yielded for the common benefit. Human hearts must be wrung with grief. The way to the kingdom lies through much tribulation. So the all-wise, all-loving God ordains. There can be no palm, no crown, without the cross. But we would look beyond the gloom and pain of dying, to the glory and the blessedness which death opens to the spirit. Ah! those who have died, really live. To-day, always, they must be near. For hearts that love each other can know no separation.

COMRADES: These were your associates in the ranks of battle and death. By God's grace you were spared the stroke that took away their lives. To-day you recall the scenes in which they were your companions. Not to-day alone, but forever you will keep their memory green. Wherever their bodies lie buried, in the soil of the land for which they died, or in the sea which giveth not up its dead, their souls have entered into victorious, peaceful life. For them the din of battle is hushed forever; for them no toiling marches, no gnawing hunger, no parching thirst, no lingering sickness, no corroding pain. "The former things have passed away," and they have entered into rest! The monument, which a grateful State has erected to their honor, passeth into your care. Around this memorial shaft, the invisible sentinels of your love will keep their constant watch and ward.

FELLOW CITIZENS: These exercises approach their termination. There is but little more to say, and what we say will soon be forgotten. But the fruits which have grown from what these men—and such as these—have done and suffered, will be the blessing of all the future of our republic. Our thoughts and life are already raised to a higher plane by the inspiration of their example. Into the heavy atmosphere of our greed and gain comes this breeze of self-sacrificing valor, and the souls of men are more erect, generous and brave. Into the easy and self-indulgent habits of life comes this spirit of cheerful endurance and self-denial, and the hearts of men are emboldened to refuse the base suggestions of a cowardly policy, and fearlessly face all evil and shameful things. Into the passions, intrigues, and ambitions of men comes the memory of this heroic story, to tell what liberty demands of her defenders, and with what honor she crowns their deeds.

This monument thus teaches the eternal lesson : HOW TO LIVE WITHOUT REPROACH, HOW TO DIE WITHOUT FEAR. So, to-day, we dedicate it to the memory of a virtue that was faithful unto death ; a valor, that accepted every extremity of danger and sacrifice ; an unselfish patriotism, in man and woman, that thought no offering too great or precious for the country's good ; a loyal self-devotion that blessed humanity far and wide. In lines of beauty, power, and grace has the artist set before us his completed work. Here it will stand through the years to come. The storms will beat upon it. The sunshine will play around it. But neither will the storm obscure, nor the sunshine brighten its glory. The rapid stream of travel and traffic will flow ceaselessly by its side. The generations will come and go. The passing years will bring their occasions of assembly, when the multitudes will gather here to find an inspiration for present duty in the recollections of a heroic past. The tear will start as the survivor of the conflict reads the inscription that speaks of some dear comrade. Mothers and fathers, sisters and wives, will search for the name of son, brother, husband, whom they gave to the country, as though they were shedding their own hearts' blood. Children will spell out these lines ; young men and maidens will whisper to each other the sad, but glorious tale ; white-haired age, with trembling lip, will repeat it, and grow young again in the remembrance ; and those who have been bereaved by the war will glory in this inheritance of lasting fame. Our own people will be quickened to a grander life, as they contemplate what is here recorded. The visitor from foreign lands will learn from it how American citizens, of every station, can do, and dare, and die, in obedience to the dictates of patriotic duty. Long after you and I have passed from the ranks of the living, and our names have been lost in forgetfulness, will this structure stand, in its simple beauty, its compact material, its undecaying granite and bronze, to teach all future generations how Rhode Island brought to the altar of the Republic her dearest sons !

Solemnly is our monument dedicated now by us. More solemnly would we, now and always, dedicate ourselves to the brave and generous patriotism, which it commemorates, and which shines out with ever increasing lustre from the names it bears!

The following Memorial Hymn was then sung :

MEMORIAL HYMN—By the Choir.

Written for the occasion by Mrs. SARAH ELLEN WHITMAN.

Music—"*Keller's American Hymn.*"

Raise the proud pillar of granite on high,
 Graced with all honors that love can impart;
Lift its fair sculptures against the blue sky,
 Blazoned and crowned with the trophies of art,—
 Crowned with the triumphs of genius and art!
  Long may its white column soar to the sky,
  Like a lone lily that perfumes the mart,
 Lifting its coronal beauty on high.

Sons of Rhode Island, your record shall stand
 Graven on tablets of granite and bronze :
Soldiers and sailors beloved of our land,
 Darlings and heroes, our brothers and sons,—
 Gray-bearded heroes and beautiful sons !
  Soldiers and sailors, the flower of our land,
  Deep, as on tablets of granite and bronze.
 Graved on our hearts shall your bright record stand.

Swell the loud psalm, let the war trumpets sound ;
 Fling the old flag to the wild Autumn blast ;
High in Valhallah our comrades are crowned,
 There may we meet when life's conflicts are past,—
 Meet in the great Hall of Heroes at last !
  High in Valhallah our comrades are crowned,
  Swell with Hosannas the wild Autumn blast !
 Let the full chorus of voices resound !

At the close of the Hymn, benediction was pronounced by
the Rev. Dr. Caswell, President of Brown University ; after
which, the Marine Artillery gave the Monument a salute.

NAMES

OF

OFFICERS, SOLDIERS AND SEAMEN

BELONGING TO THE

State of Rhode Island,

WHETHER SERVING IN RHODE ISLAND REGIMENTS, IN THE REGIMENTS OF OTHER STATES, OR IN THE ARMY AND NAVY OF THE UNITED STATES.

WHO LOST THEIR LIVES IN DEFENCE OF THEIR COUNTRY DURING THE LATE REBELLION.

———

ENGRAVED ON BRONZE TABLETS ON THE SOLDIERS' AND SAILORS' MONUMENT IN PROVIDENCE.

General and Staff Officers.

Maj.-Gen. Isaac I. Stevens, Brigadier-Gen. Isaac P. Rodman, Lieutenant Robert H. Ives, Jun'r.

First Regiment Rhode Island Infantry.

2d Lieut. H. A. Prescott.　　　Serg't. Jas. H. Peckham,
Corp. Sam. Foster, 2d.

Arnold, John Rice
Ackley, Wm. H.
Bolton, Thos.
Burdick, A. H.
Clarke, John A.
Comstock, Jessie
Dexter, Fred A.
Downs, Paul,
Dougherty, Jas.
Danforth, Sam. C.
Davis, Henry C.
Deblois, S. D.
Flagg Geo. W.

Falvey, John
Hawkins, W. D.
Harrington, Thos. Jr.
Harrop, John
Knowles, Frank H.
Luther, H. H.
Melville, Hugh
Penno, A. B.
Peckham, J. P.
Quirk, Mathew
Remington, H. H.
Schocher, Herman
Tillinghast, H. L.

White, A. J.

2d Rhode Island Infantry.

Col. John S. Slocum,
Maj. Sullivan Ballou,
Capt. Jos. E. McIntyre,
Capt. Levi Tower,
Capt. S. James Smith,
Capt. Edwin K. Sherman,

Capt. John P. Shaw,
Capt. Chas. W. Gleason,
Capt. Thorndike J. Smith,
1st Lieut. Thos. H. Carr,
1st Lieut. Wm. H. Perry,
2nd Lieut. Clarke E. Bates.

Sergeants.

Chas. E. Bagley,
E. J. Blake,
H. T. Blanchard,
Henry J. Cole,
B. Chamberlain,
Jas. H. Coyle,
Henry A. Greene,
Caleb B. Kent,
Jas. A. King,

S. E. Moon,
Jas. A. Nichols,
S. A. Newman,
Jas. E. Stanley,
Jas. Seamans,
Henry L. Taft,
James Taylor,
Paul Visser,
Wm. C. Webb,

Sam. Wight.

Corporals.

Wm. P. Bentley,
Thos H. Barker,
John Burk,
T. O. H. Carpenter,

John W. Hunt,
Thos. I. Kelley,
S. T. Matteson,
Jas. Mansell,

Corporals.

P. Carrol,   Alex. Mills,
A. F. Davis,   Noah A. Peck,
John Ford,   Sam. T. Perry,
Thos. H. B. Fales,   Joel E. Rice,
W. B. Gray,   Geo. H. Reed,
R. M. Grant,   F. C. Ronan,
F. C. Greene.   Fred. W. Swain,
J. G. Grinnell,   Esek C. Smith,
Jas. T. Glancy,   Benj. W. Sherman,
T. A. Goldsmith,   Stephen Shaw,
Stephen Holland,   Job Tanner,
Chas. A. Haile,   D. E. Valett,
                    Lewis B. Wilson.

Privates.

Armstrong, James   Graves, Sam. W.
Allen, Geo. M.   Gibson, Daniel
Alger, Mathew   Hunter, A. B.
Arnold, Leander A.   Hunt, Joseph
Arnold, Wm. A.   Hall, John C.
Aldrich, Wilson   Himes, Albert
Atwood, Geo. B.   Hennessey, Thomas.
Brennan, John J.   Heavey, Patrick
Blair, John   Hunt, Job H.
Bartlett, Reuben   Island, Patrick
Burns, Wm. B.   Jordan, Jas. B.
Brayton, G. J.   Jacques, Henry L.
Barton, Jos.   Johnson, Jas. G.
Bailey, John   Jordan, William
Butler, Jas. D.   Lawton, H. C.
Cole, Alfred C.   Lawton, A. W.
Cooper, Thomas   Lawton, J. F.
Cob, Isaac N.   Littlefield, Wm. D.
Card, Peleg W.   Lewis, Jas. E.
Calligan, Jas.   Luther, Jerry Jr.
Davis, Henry M.   Landy, John
Dugan, James   Lewis, Thos.
Dean, John E.   Matteson, H. G.
Donnovan, John   Marsden, George
Dagnan, Thos.   Miner, Chris. A.
Dewhurst, J. W.   Medbury, Wm. H.
Ehlert, Ludwig   McCabe, J.
Earle, John   Murphy, P. J.
Fay, Michael   McLane, A.
Farrell, John   Marland, H.
Farrell, John   Maxfield, Geo. H.
Franklin, Aug. B.   Martin, James
Fahey, John   Mowry, Daniel
Greene, William   Morse, Ed. T.
Greene, Daniel   McCann, Wm. J.
Greene, Geo. W.   Mullen, P. J.
Greene, Richard   Malcolm, Hugh

McKay, Thomas. 2d.
McElroy, John
Mowry, Charles F.
McCabe, John
Nichols, Wm. H.
Nicholson, J. C.
Newman. D. A.
Powers, Chas.
Phillips, Joseph A.
Reynolds, Wm. E.
Rodman, Isaac C.
Records, Wm. H.
Railton, Wm.
Rice, John
Randall, Wm. H.
Randal, I. C.
Russell, Samuel
Spencer, John
Shaw, L. R.
Smith Geo. H.
Stetson, Albert
Slocum John H.
Simmons, Ed. A.
Sweet, Sam. P. Jr.

Stone, A. H.
Sheldon, Walter M.
Smith, Anson J.
Shane, Robert
Strange, H. A.
Smith, James
Slocum, Henry
Sullivan, Timothy
Spencer, R. A.
Taylor, John H.
Tibbits, H. C.
Toye, Robert
Thurber, D. N
Tupper, Charles R.
Tucker, Chas. W.
Tarbox, Benj.
Tourgee, Alonzo
Vose, C. F.
Vatelacaici, Jos.
Warren, W. F.
Wilson, John A.
Wilcox, Geo. W.
Winsor, Pitts S.
Wilcox, Caleb
Whipple, Ethan Jr.

3rd R. I. Heavy Artillery.

Col. Nat'l W. Brown,
1st. Lieut. Fred. Metcalf,
1st Lieut. George Carpenter,
1st Lieut. E. W. Keene,
1st Lieut. H. Holbrook,
2nd Lieut. E. S. Bartholomew,
2nd Lieut. Walter B. Manton.

Sergeants.

J. J. Carpenter, Jr.　　　George J. Hill,　　　Martin Heeney.

Corporals.

J. N. Bogman,
Wm. Cody,
Thos. Miner,
F. S. Peck,
Chas. D. Stalker,
Chas. W. Weeden,
I. H. Pinckney.

Privates.

Arnold, Dan. L.
Angell, H. S.
Abby, Charles
Brown, George
Brown, Wm. L.
Burdick, F. E.
Brayton, Benj. F.
Barbour, Jas. D.

Hughes, Joseph
Howe, M. S.
Ide, A. D.
Jagneth, George W.
Jefferson, George
Joslin, Edward
Kelly, James
Kallaher, P.

7

Privates.

Burnes, M.
Burroughs, William
Burk, Patrick
Brophy, William
Briggs, Daniel B.
Bullock, John S.
Case Nat. N.
Crosby, Daniel
Crosby, E. H.
Chace, Benjamin
Crowley, James
Chaffee, W.
Conoly, P.
Campbell, Thomas
Conboy, Henry
Carroll, Henry
Carroll, F.
Diggle, Daniel
Dunn, John
Doherty, Thomas
Davis William
Dexter, George R.
Dunbar, E.
Egan, R.
Elwell, Noel
Eddy, Warren
Fallow, John
Farrell, L.
Farrer, Wm.
Fiske, Emery
Fish, Joseph H.
Greenhalch, Wm. J.
Gunter, Daniel
Gibbons, M. I.
Gorton, John A.
Gannon, P.
Gilligan, P. H.
Golden, Daniel
Grimes, John I.
Goodwin, George F.
Harrington, D. T.
Horton, E. R. M.
Hyde, John
Havens, Jas. D.
Harris, James
Hickes, Geo. W.
Hackett, Edward

Ketchum, A. S.
Luther, Joseph T.
Lambe, John
Leonard, A. L.
Moon, H. N.
McQuillin, F.
Malone, D.
Morgan, Charles
McCool, John
McKenzie, Alex. R.
Mowry, M. B.
McGahan, James
Monroe, Chas. H.
Megan, M.
Murray, B.
McKenna, John
Mace, George W.
Nailan, Peter
O'Sullivan, James
O'Donnell, James
Prew, M.
Potter, I. A.
Rice, George
Rounds, Chas. H.
Riley, Thomas
Ryan, Thomas
Ryan. James
Smith, Geo. W.
Smith, L. R.
Saunders, A. B.
Stewart. John E.
Stayles, Benj. L.
Sweet, Sam. S.
Smith, David
Stewart, S. H.
Tillinghast, Wm. C.
Tanner, Thos. B.
Turnbull, Thos. W.
Thornton, M. G.
Taft, F. H.
Valleley, E. J.
Warner, John B.
Wright, R. P.
Worden, W. H.
Warfield, H. H.
Wells, B. S.
Welsh, Harry

4th R. I. Infantry.

Lieut. Col. Jos. B. Curtis,
Quartermaster Brayton Knight,
Capt. Chas. H. Tillinghast,
Ass't. Surg. G. J. Smalley.

2d Lieut. John K. Knowles,
2d Lieut. George W. Field,
2d Lieut. James T. Farley.

Sergeants.

George R. Buffum,
George H. Church, Jr.
Charles E. Guild,
Gustavus B. Gardner,

Charles A. Gorton,
C. P. Myrick,
J. N. Parker,
Fred. J. Peabody,

Alexander Sanford.

Corporals.

Benjamin F. Burdick,
Thomas Bloomer,
Byron W. Dyer,
William S. Denham,
James Grinrod,
Samuel Harvey,
R. Hayden,

H. V. Hopkins,
John Hayes,
T. A. Langworthy,
H. R. Thayer,
Thomas B. Tanner,
George S. Thomas,
W. P. Wilcox.

Privates.

Austin, Jacob
Anthony, Wm. J.
Abbott, A. J. W.
Bumpers, S.
Bunn, Daniel,
Burus, Timothy
Bane, Wm. H.
Burdick, S. M.
Bliss Samuel D.
Boss, Daniel A.
Baker, Charles C.
Brownell, W. D.
Briggs, Charles H.
Ballou, George E.
Collum, George
Card, Jonathan,
Cameron, D. H.
Chapman, H.
Clark, John T.
Crandall, D.
Costigan, C.
Carr, Wm. H.
Chase, John W.
Curtis, Samuel
Chaill, Nathaniel,
Durgan, P.
Dailey, Daniel
Davis, James

Donnegan H.
Davis, Chas. E.
Edgers, E.
Fitzgerald J.
Frisby, Silas
Fish, Henry
Gardiner, Wm. H.
Gallagher, P.
Gavitt, E. D.
Gladding, H, F.
Hopkins, Allen
Hardman, R.
Harday, John
Healy, Thaddeus,
Henry, John
Harrington, J.
Hopkins, Wm. S.
Hopkins, A. B.
Horton, J. B.
Johnson, Philip
Johnson, Elijah
Jefferson, James W.
Jenens, Nelson
Johnson, J. F.
Kenworthy, R.
Kelley, George W.
Kelley, George A.
Kettle, Charles

Privates.

Landers, James H.
Lyons, Thomas
Lake, Thomas C.
Lynch, Edward
Livsey, Theodore
McNeal, P.
McDonald Edward
Myrick, Samuel
Moon, Josiah
Martin, George
McGowan, William
McNamee, H. M.
Miller, Wm. A.
Murphy, John
McCabe M.
McKee, Andrew
Mattison, J. A.
Manchester, Thomas
McCandles, R.
Murphy, C.
O'Marra, Thomas
Oliver, Joseph
Pike, Ephraim
Rathbun, L. W.
Roe, Jacob
Roberts, Henry
Ready, John

Randall, James
Reynolds, A. F.
Remington, A. J.
Shakshalf, George
Sheridan, P.
Stacey, M. E.
Steere, Willard
Staples, A. H.
Saunders, H. F.
Street, Edwin
Stafford, Wm. E.
Simmons, Lloyd
Sherman, Edward E.
Tew, William
Thornton, Augustus T.
Tripp, Alden
Tourtelott, Reuben
Tyler, Archibald A.
Tyler, Edwin
Tew, Richard T.
Tourjee, J. F.
Wood, George M.
Williams, R.
Walker, James
Winterbottom, J.
Weaver, Benoni
Weaver, Alton J.

5th R. I. Heavy Artillery.

Quartermaster M. H. Gladding, ·
Quartermaster Wm. W. Prouty,
Quartermaster C. E. Lawton,
Capt. James Gregg,
Capt. Joseph McIntyre,

1st Lieut. Wm. W. Hall,
1st Lieut. H. R. Pierce,
1st Lieut. Geo. F. Turner,
2d Lieut. Charles E. Beers.

Sergeants.

Samuel R. Eddy,
Thomas Hanley,

M. Kennedy,
L. V. Ludwig,

Charles Perrigo.

Corporals.

E. O. Colvin,
Charles H. Eddy,
John George,
J. M. Gallagher,

S. H. Grimwood,
W. W. Paull,
M. Riley,
Charles A. Slocum.

Privates.

Allen, John M.
Bane, Frederick
Brady, James

Boss, Edward F.
Brown, John
Ballou, Dennis G.

Privates.

Brown, John
Bugbee, L. W.
Barnes Samuel A.
Bourne, I. D.
Collins, Thomas
Copeland, Charles
Campbell, D.
Chace, Charles F.
Clark, Charles C.
Callahan, P.
Chase, F. R.
Cooney, Thomas
Delaney, Charles
Doyle, James
Doolittle, George L.
Dean, George B.
Devin, Charles
Eaton Amos
Eddy, James M.
Farrell, P.
Fee, Arthur
Flood, John
Frazier, R.
Fielding, P.
Goudy, John
Garvey, William
Green, John
Gardner, Thadeus
Gould, E. A.
Greenup, I. W.
Hampstead, J.
Hawkins, D. F.
Hornby, John
Hopkins, George W.
Haskell, A. Jr.
Henry, Lewis,
Hill, Smith
Hanes, Pasco, Jr.
Hait, M.
Ivars, Daniel
Johnson, A. J.
Johnson, Charles
Keleghan, C.
Lee, Cornelius

Livingston, John
Lillibridge, Wm. H.
Lewis, Edward,
Lawton, Wm. J.
Liscomb, B. D.
McLaughlin James
Montgomery, George
Murphy, J.
Miller, John
Miller, John
McElroy P.
McDonald, D.
Norris T.
O'Leary, P.
Peck, James E.
Peck Edwin B.
Rourke, P.
Ryan, Thomas
Ryan, John
Redding, George
Ryan, William
Ryan, Patrick
Sanders, Charles
Seymour H.
Sisson, Charles S.
Sullivan, Jerry
Smith, Samuel
Simmons, James
Stewart, Charles
Shippy, Thomas
Sherman, Amos B.
Smith, George
Schmidt, Louis
Thomas, John
Tracy, Christopher
Vallett, Wm. H.
Wickes, Stephen
Wicks, Franklin
Wallace, William
Wilson, Jerry
Wilson, B.
Wright, Thomas
White, Emery
Williams, John, 1st.
Weed, M.

7th R. I. Infantry.

Lieut. Col. W. B. Sayles,
Lieut. Col. Job Arnold,
Major Jacob Babbitt,
Bt. Major P. E. Peckham,
Capt. James N. Potter,

1st Lieut. A. L. Smith,
1st Lieut. A. A. Bowles,
2d Lieut. C. H. Kellen,
Lieut. Samuel McIlroy.

Sergeants.

George W. Congdon,
Darius J. Cole,
M. Flaherty,
Wm. Harrington,
John K. Hull,

Charles A. Knowles,
H. L. Morse,
Joseph S. Sweet,
James B. Spencer.
D. B. Westcott,
William T. Wood.

Corporals.

P. Bridgehouse,
R. B. Briggs,
Samuel G. Brown,
Samuel O. Follett,
A. H. Howarth,
John E. Hopkins,
A. A. Lillibridge,
John McDevitt,
Joseph A. Marcoux,
Isaac Nye,

Manuel, Open
O. Phillips,
F. W. Potter,
Charles Rhowarts,
Samuel E. Rice,
D. B Sherman,
S. F. Simpson,
George H. Smith,
L. Whitcomb,
O. A. Whitman,

Privates.

Austin, Benj. K.
Adams, S. G.
Alexander H.
Austin, W. G.
Albro, Edmund B.
Arnold, Benjamin F.
Arnold, Reuben
Ashworth William
Bentley, Wm.
Battey, Hiram S.
Burdick, Joseph W.
Bitgood, Joseph H.
Budlong, Benjamin
Boyles, Charles
Brown, A. G.
Brown. J. F.
Burdick, W. C.
Bacon James H.
Barber, Jesse N.
Barber, Israel A.
Brayman, Henry
Browning, O. N.
Ballou, George E.

Burke, John
Butman, George
Clark, John B.
Collins, G. F.
Crane, Thomas
Caswell, Alfred
Cox, William
Coman, Wm. A.
Colvin, N. D.
Cahoone, Sylvester
Chater, Joseph
Cameron, Uz
Champlin, C. E.
Clark, J. R.
Cornell, Martin
Cornell, Ira B.
Collins. Wm.
Corbin, A. N.
Cole, Henry S.
Corey Charles K.
Clark, Stephen A.
Dorrance, John
Durfee, Gilbert

Privates.

Dempster, John
Essex, Richard
Eddy, John S.
Ferrey, James
Franklin, C. L.
Findley, Wm.
Franklin, J.
Farrow, Enos
Field, George A.
Gardiner, George W.
Gorton, Joel B.
Greene, Chas. B.
Greene, Wm. H.
Grant, Ira W.
Gallagher, Owen
Gilfoil, P.
Gardner, Chas. W.
Greene, Robert B.
Gorton, Richard, Jr.
Gardiner, Chas. W.
Gladding, James H.
Gardner, F. H.
Hughes, James
Hadfield, R.
Harrah, Oliver O.
Holbrook, Joseph H.
Hunt, Benj. S.
Healey, H. D.
Hodson, James
Hall, Wm. A.
Hathaway, A. P.
Holloway, Thomas T
Hopkins, John
Hopkins, Asel A.
Hopkins, Wm. D.
Hopkins, D. A.
Johnson, W. H.
Kenyon, Thomas R.
Kenyon, James G.
Kettle, Chas. A.
Kenyon, Joseph J.
Knight, Alfred S.
Kelley, Patrick
Kenyon, A. D.
Knight, Thomas
Kenyon, John C.
Kenyon, Thomas G.
Kilroy, John
Lewis, John D.
Lynch, John
Leary, Jerry
Ledden, Daniel
McKenna, Owen

Malone, John
Maloy, Thomas
McCaslin, Thomas
Mathewson, N. W.
May, Elisha G.
Manchester, Alex. H.
Maxon, Joel C.
Manchester, Isaac B.
Niles, Nelson
O'Neil, James
Olney, Zalmon A.
Pierce, Christopher R.
Pierce, Allen
Pelan, Robert T.
Philips, E. B.
Perkins, P. B.
Pate, Wm.
Pierce, H. N.
Pollock, Wm. J.
Place, Arnold J.
Peckham, Benjamin
Potter, Roswell H.
Rowen, Thomas
Ratcliffe, R.
Robbins, N. N.
Rose, George P.
Rose, Robert N.
Rathburn, N.
Rice, John E.
Read, Frank E.
Reynolds, E. S.
Saunders, I. N.
Spencer, Wm. H.
Steere, John F.
Sweetland, Job R.
Steere, Benoni
Sisson, Benjamin F.
Spencer, John
Strait, P. P.
Sisson, Randall
Smith, R. D.
Smith, Daniel
Snow, Samuel, Jr.
Smith, Thomas E.
Simmons, George
Turner, Chas.
Thomas, George A.
Taylor, Edwin
Trainor, M.
Tourjee, Wm.
Taylor, S. J.
Taylor, James J.
Underwood, P. G.

Privates.

Worden, Charles H.
Whipple, Olney
Willis, Abel, Jr.

Winsor, A. A.
Wood, Oliver
Whitman, R. A.
Wright, H. C.

9th R. I. Infantry.

Corp. Hollis Tabor, Jr.

Privates.

Arnold, S. B.   Simonds, Joseph N.

10th R. I. Infantry.

Privates.

Atwood, Wm. F.   Meggett, M. McA.

10th R. I. Light Battery.

Corp. James Flait.

11th R. I. Infantry

Hosp. Steward, I. S. Pervear, Jr.   Corp. Isaac H. Pickney.

Privates.

Atwood, William
Bliss, F. M.
Clarke, B. W.
Carpenter, J. M.
Chrystol, Charles P.

Gould, E. F.
Horton, R.
Northup, G.
Phinney, John D.
Wyman, Wm. J.

12th R. I. Infantry.

1st Lieut. R. A. Briggs,
1st Lieut. Jas. M. Pendleton, 2d,

1st Lieut. Stephen M. Hopkins
Private P. McDermott.

Sergeants.

George W. Arnold,
Samuel Babcock,

J. G. Davis,
Isaac Gorham.

Corporals.

A. H. Bennett,   L. C. Huntington,   Lorenzo Stow.

Privates.

Austin, George H.
Bailey, Thomas W.
Brennan, Hugh
Ball, William

Bennett, A. J.
Burns, Michael
Bishop, M. V. B.
Bucklin, George

Privates.

Buxton, A. A.
Caswell, John
Conley, Daniel W.
Chissold, Stephen
Crandall, D. A.
Cahoone, Charles H.
Connelly, Terry
Dorsey, John
Duffy, John C.
Gifford, Russell
Grinnell, A.
Gorton, Jacob
Greene, Clark
Humphrey H. N.
Jenckes, J. E.
Kinnicutt, Geo R. Jr.
Keeler, R. N.
Lawson, John
Lewis, James G.
Meyers, Samuel A.
Mason, William
Mitchell, Jesse D.

Mitchell, David
Miller, Nathan L.
McArthur, John
Pearce. Henry W.
Paine, E. A. J.
Richardson, George E.
Richmond George W.
Spink, George T.
Smith, Benj. R.
Sprague, Civilian
Sheldon, John
Salisbury, A. F.
Strait, Oliver C.
Tinkham, Thomas
Tew, James
Tourjee, George R.
Wood, George W.
Whiting, Samuel S.
Whitman, Hiram
Wilbur, Edward J.
Wilder, Frank
Webb, Charles A.

Williams, G. O.

Hospital Guards.

Privates.

Carr, Stephen A.
Higgins, John

Tanner, Charles H.
Taylor, John

14th R. I. Heavy Artillery, (Colored.)

Capt. Henry Simon,
Capt. A. R. Rawson,

1st Lieut. John E. Wardlow,
2d Lieut. James P. Brown,

2d Lieut. Charles W. Monroe.

Sergeants.

A. Atwood,
H. F. Davis,
H. F. Davis,
L. J. Fry,
M. Graham,
S. R. Jarvis,
Willis Jones,

Samuel Mason,
Wm. H. Mann,
Simon Niles,
John Pell,
Joseph Smith,
Isaac Smedus.
Josiah Walker.

Corporals.

C. Anderson,
J. E. Brown.
J. M. Brown,
William Chace,

J. W. Cartwright,
A. G. Freeman,
B. C. Gardner,
Wm. L. Humbert.

Corporals.

L. E. Hicks,
A. G. Jackson,
I. R. Lowe,

Henry Mason,
Charles H. Moore,
H. J. Thompson.

Privates.

Allen, R. B.
Anson, L.
Abbott, Wm. L.
Anthony J.
Anthony, L. G.
Allen H.
Banks, H.
Babcock I.
Bayard, J.
Brister, A. W.
Bush, H.
Bush, William
Butler, John
Bell, John
Baker, L.
Brown, J. W.
Brewster, A.
Benson, L. G. M.
Boardley, James
Barrett, A.
Betson, William
Barrett, H.
Brown, George W.
Coleman, J. L.
Cisco, Charles
Charles, John
Corson, J.
Cheese, T. S.
Carr, S.
Clark, J.
Clayton, C. L.
Cambridge, W. H.
Carter, W. H.
Claxton, R.
Cox, E. A.
Clare, Austin
Cummings, F.
Cæsar, R.
Copeland, A.
Cole, P.
Carroll, D.
Clay, William
Cleggett, W. F.
Congdon, James
Davis, A.
Degroot, D.
Dubois, H.

Demming, Wm.
Dailey, Gus.
DeMars, G.
Demon, J.
Dolphin, James
Dusenbury, L.
Derrick, Wm. P.
Denny, W.
Detew, H.
Debois, T. B.
Dewitt, Wm.
Dorsey, J. H.
Everson, P.
Edwards, N,
Edwards, D.
Elkley, A. E.
Ellis, Charles H.
Eris, T. O.
Freeman, Charles
Fry, James,
Fisher, L.
Freeman, A. J.
Frazier, J. H.
Furber, N.
Fletcher, Samuel
Fisher, F.
Fletcher, D. R.
Fletcher, R. L.
Fairfax, T. C.
Fletcher, W.
Gardner, W. C.
Gardner, H. J.
Greene, A.
Gaines, John
Grames, F. C.
Geer, H.
Gardner, J. C.
Giles, James,
Grant, William A.
Green, George
Gibson, E. H.
Gordon, John
Greene, John
Good, H.
Greer, R.
Griffin, Charles
Griffin, H. A.

Privates.

Gardner, H. F.
Huntington, H.
Hamblin, J. P.
Hector, Wm. H.
Hollis, R.
Hallam, C. H.
Hill, James
Holmes, N.
Holmes, Thomas
Harris, Wm. H.
Hicks, J. J.
Hogan, F.
Hinkman, J.
Hagamore, George
Harris, C. W.
Hopper, B. H.
Harway, P. A.
Hawes, Alexander
Henson, Joseph
Hicks, P.
Hazel, A.
Hardy, C. H.
Haird, J.
Henry, J.
Hall, Nat.
Henry, James F.
Hill, H. C.
Honeycutt, G.
Hornbeck, T.
Howland, George
Irons, R.
Irving, William
Isaac, J.
Jackson, William H.
Johnson, George H.
Jackson, D.
Jackson, T.
Jackson, William C.
Jackson, James M.
Jackson, L.
Jackson, L.
Johnson, E.
Jones, A.
Jones George W.
Jones M.
Jackson, E.
Jackson, S.
Jackson, Samuel
Jackson, Ad.
Jones Wm.
Jefferson, S. O.
Jones, Ed. James

Judson. Thomas
Johnson, Charles H.
Johnson, P. H.
Johnson, Joseph W.
Johnson, John
Jones, James F.
King Corn'l.
Kellman, James H.
King, A.
Keller, John
Kenney, John
Kenney, William
Laws, Leoni
Lippitt, George
Lunn, Amos A.
Lenisen, P.
Lambert, A
Lee, John
Lewis, Jesse
Lucas, James
Labiel, Wm. H.
Lee. John W.
Lonks, J. A.
Lee, Henry
Miltier, Solomon
Martin, Thomas
Merrick, John
Moody, Joseph
Mason, Isaac
Moore, Charles C.
McClow, James
Mix, Collins
McCarty, H.
Mason, Samuel
Mann, Stephen
Mills, Wm. W.
Miller, Benjamin
Morton, W.
McGill, William
Morrison, William A.
Moore, George
Myers, A. C.
Nosa, J.
Niles, E. F.
Norris, George
Nite, Joseph T.
Newcomb, Wm. W.
Nelson, Charles C. 2d,
Outland, M.
Proffit, C. M.
Potter, F. A.
Pierce, G. W.

Privates.

Paine, V.
Powers, J.
Page, P.
Palmer, O.
Peters, J. W.
Peterson, W.
Peters, C. H.
Paine, A.
Poole F.
Beynolds, Edward
Rooms, J.
Rhodes, J.
Ricks, H.
Ricks, S. I,
Reed, C. P.
Randall, H.
Randall R.
Reynolds, A.
Robblns, William
Reading, S.
Redder, J. W.
Rich, John
Randle, J. B.
Roberts, C. A.
Scott, N.
Stephens, Thomas
Smith, J. M.
Smith, B. F.
Sullivan, J.
Smothers, F.
Saunders, J.
Smith, James
Smith D.
Steward, E. A.
Staunton. W. J.
Sills, E. H.
Scott, J. W.
Smith E.
Stevenson, R. M.
Scudder, Wm. G.
Simms, J. W.
Sanford, James
Seaton, George
Smith, J.
Smith, A. E.
Seman, E.
Simons, J.
Simons, Wm. H.
Somersét, L.

Smith, L. H.
Saunders, A.
Tembroke, S.
Telegrove, J.
Tuttle, S.
Townsend, D.
Tossett, C. J.
Thom, F.
Townsend, J.
Thomas, John
Tierce, S. A.
Thomas, James
Talbot, P. W.
Thomas, Judson
Terrell, R.
Valentine. J. S.
Weeden, Charles
Warmsley, James
Warmsley, D.
Williams. E.
Wallace, George
Williams. H.
Williams, R.
Wilson, S. H.
Williams. M.
Wilson, A. D.
Woods, Samuel
Williams, A.
Weddinston, J. H.
Welden, Stephen
West, Wm. H.
Woolsey, A.
Watts, George E.
Williamson, T.
West Job
Wycoff, T. A.
Walker, James
Warren, John
White W.
White, A. T.
Washington, George
Washington, Wm.
Wheatley, Joshua
Winn, A.
Williams, Edward
Wells, R.
Watkins, S. L.
Whitfield, J. H.
Young, Samuel

Youter, James R.

1st R. I. Light Artillery.

Bt. Capt. Charles V. Scott,
1st. Lieut. Peter Hunt,
2d Lieut. Benjamin Kelley,
2d Lieut. Joseph S. Milne,
2d Lieut. Francis A. Smith.

Sergeants.

Charles H. Adams,
George P. Carpenter,
Benjamin H. Draper,
John T. Greene,
Aug. S. Hanna,
Charles H. Kimball,
Jacob F. Kent,
F. S. Moies,
A. A. Phillips,
George A. Perry,
Charles M. Read,
Albert Straight,
E. G. Sullivan.

Corporals.

H. H. Ballou,
James A. Cole,
H. E. Chase,
William A. Dickerson,
George A. Eldred,
William Hamilton,
Otis F. Hicks,
Wm. Jones,
N. T. Morse, Jr.
J. B. Mathewson,
Benjamin F. Martindale,
?. C. Olney,
Earnest Simpson,
William M. Tanner,
William B. Thompson,
A. H. Trescott,
A. A. Walker,
George H. Watson.

Privates.

Austin, George R.
Arnold, H. N.
Bosworth, Joseph T.
Bubb, Frederick M.
Bourn, William E.
Brown, F. A.
Burton, H. W.
Burton, Joseph C.
Burt, Everett B.
Brannan, John
Beard, William
Railey, Wm. H.
Benway, Thomas
Bartlett, John E.
Baxter, H. H.
Braman, James H.
Bowen, George W.
Booth, James
Chaffee, George W.
Church, N. L.
Clark, Charles
Cæsar, Daniel
Carroll, Edward
Collins, William
Colvin, John
Colwell, A. N.
Conner, James
Conneng, John
Coffey, M.
Carrigan, P.
Carter, Thomas
Dennis, William
Donnohoe, H.
Doran, Hugh
Davis, William M.
Dailey, David
Davis, James C.
Douglas, J. W.
Easterbrooks, S.
Flynn, M.
Fox, Samuel W.
French, Joseph S.
Fisk, George W.
Fiske, Charles D.
Fenner, George D.
Gladding, O. D.
Gardner, Alfred
Greene, C. H. H.
Green, John
Glynn, John
Galloughly, J.
Galvin, Edward

Privates.

Greene, L. A.
Gavitt. James L.
Goff. A. B.
Gardner, Charles G.
Goff, Thomas J.
Hazleton, Edgar
Hendrick, A. E.
Hunt, C. F.
Holden, George W.
Hewett, Henry
Ham, George W.
Harvey M.
Harrop, Joseph
Higgins, George
Hazard, Job
Healey, Wm. B.
Hall, Henry
Horton, A. C.
Horton, H. R.
Horton, James H.
Johnson, J. H.
King, David B.
King, William H.
Kenyon, W. W.
Lawrence, J. H.
Lannegan, P.
Luther, Joseph
Lamphear, Thomas F.
La Fount, Louis
Levins, M. M.
Larkins, R. E.
Lewis, W. H.
Lannehan P.
Marcy, A. W.
Moran, John
Moffett, Thomas
Montgomery, F. E.
Mullen, F.
McNeigh, H.
McGovern, John
Moore, Charles
Morris, M. M.
Mason, Wm.
McCafferey, Edward
Medbury, L. A.
Matteson, E. A.
McComb, John
McCabe, P.
Mars, T. F.
McManus, C.
Manter, Wm. G.
Nason, Henry

Norris, B. J.
Nesbitt, Wm.
Nye, J. R.
O'Brien, P.
O'Rourke, John
Peckham. Wm. S.
Pickett, Erastus
Pratt, James F.
Potter, Elisha
Pomeroy, E.
Phillips, John
Reynolds, John T.
Ryan Daniel
Rose, Richard
Rathbone, J. L.
Slocum, M. F.
Stone, Edwin
Salisbury, Wm.
Swain, R. C.
Seamans, E. W.
Sanford, H D.
Swan, John J. E.
Slaver, John
Sayles, C A.
Sullivan, C.
Sutcliffe, R.
Stanley, Milton
Sulpaugh, J. H,
Stephens, G. W.
Shiny, H.
Trescott, J. F. Jr.
Terry, David,
Thursby, S.
Thayer, B. D.
Testen, H. E.
Travers, A. F.
Traff, John
Turuer, Andrew
Tracey, George E.
Tracey. Charles
Vose, W. L.
Vaslett, Charles
Worsley, Hiram B.
Wilcox, H. B.
Winsor, W. W.
Ward, Joseph, L.
Webb, Edward J.
Watson, C. H.
Whitman, Benjamin
Wilbor, W. B.
Williams, J. L.
Young, E. S.

Zimala, John

1st R. I. Cavalry.

Capt. Wm. P. Ainsworth,
2d Lieut. Joseph A. Chedel, Jr.
2d Lieut. James P. Taylor,
2d Lieut. Charles A. Sawyer,
Lieut. L. D. Grove,
2d Lieut. H. L. Nicolai,
2d Lieut. George T. Slocum,
Q. M. Serg't. George W. Harris.

Sergeants.

John A. Austin,
John S. Brown,
R. Barrows,
Charles B. Delanah,
J. Fitzgerald,
George P. Streeter.

Corporals.

Thomas Burton,
George W. Gorton,
E. P. Gardner,
J. C. Kiernan,
Allen R. Paine,
J. R. Peterson,
George T. Reynolds,
Joseph W. Vincent.

Privates.

Allen, Henry A.
Angell, Jesse W.
Allen, Charles N.
Bates, E. B.
Burke, James
Bowditch, Isaac
Brown, William
Bidmead, William J.
Burke, James
Conlin, John
Carpenter, P.
Collins, James H.
Durden Robert
Foster, Horatio
Freelove, H. B.
Foster, Jacob B.
Graves, Charles A.
Gardner, Joseph W.
Greene, Henry
Greene, A. C.
Gould, Charles E.
Hunt, Caleb W.
Hall, T. A. G.
Healy, Alonzo
Hill, Ambrose B.
Henry, Thomas
Hammell, John
Hughes, P.
Hook, A. Von
Hiscox, Benjamin
Haine, Charles H.
Ide, S. R.
Kenyon, John
Kenyon, Charles
Kiernan, John
King, R. E.
Kettle, James
Laveran, P.
Leach, L. D.
Mulvey, John
Miner, Stephen
McGrath, P. 1st
Millington, J. W.
Northup, E.
Pette, David
Peck, J. F.
Potter, Gerge D.
Rawcliffe, J. W.
Rathbone, Jeremiah
Reynolds, Owen
Rounds, P. J.
Read, Asa K.
Smith, P. B.
Salisbury, S.
Sweet, M. W.
Shord, Joseph
Smyth, Cyrus
Sutton, E. B.
Sheridan, John
Spink, D. C.
Travers, Frank
Thompson, L.
Winsor, John
Wilcox, George S.
Wilcox, Samuel
West, Hiram
West, George W.
York, Isaac F.

2d R. I. Cavalry.

Qr. Mast. Serg't. Chas. H. Kennon,   Serg't. F. C. Ewins.

Privates.

Allen, H. F.
Beese, William M.
Brown, Charles
Davis, William
Ewin, Thomas
Eaton, Charles
Gibson, George F.
Hillman, D.

Little, S. B.
Lemann, R.
Meagann, E.
Neagal, James
Saltonstall, R.
Sherman, C.
Smith, Charles
Smith, R. F.

Wright, M.

3rd R. I. Cavalry.

Capt. Henry C. Fitts,
1st. Lieut. Albert Clapp,
1st Lieut. William A. Teft,

Lieut. James A. Wade,
1st. Lieut. Wm. E. Peck,
2d Lieut. C. D. Hammett,

Serg't. Maj. P. M. Sullivan.

Sergeants.

William A. Fiske,
Mattias Gannon,
W. E. Goodenough,
J. H. Hawkins,
H. S. Keith,
James McCormack,

Aug. Mowry,
John McCarthy,
John N. Parker,
William Swan,
H. A. Sunderland,
John Sullivan,

Ezra A. Tennant.

Corporals.

William Burnet,
Philip Cain,
I. A. Cleveland,
James L. Douglass,
S. W. Ellis,
Peter Gilroy,
Edward Logue,
S. Loeffler,

L. T. Moffit,
Charles Murray,
T. M. Magee,
Amos Perry,
N. J. Sweetland,
Charles H. Symonds,
Nathaniel Spinney,
William H. Wilcox,

William H. Walker.

Privates.

Angell, S. A.
Alexander, S. A.
Barton, Lewis
Baggs, N. D.
Brown, P. B.
Burrows, Simeon A.
Bowen, Frank
Brown, William A.
Bleavins, William A.

Benford, Augustus
Benedict, Joseph B.
Brown, C. M.
Barnes, N. K.
Brenno, Alexander
Brown, Henry
Connelly, John
Carolin, Thomas
Commerford, P.

Privates.

Clarke, J. H.
Cleverly, E.
Cleverly, J. M. Jr.
Cooke, Joseph
Chaffee, Wm. H.
Carr, Isaac
Coyne, Patrick
Cammel, Frederick
Devlin, John
Dolan, Patrick
Dodge, John T.
Drown, W. A.
Devine, B.
Dumply L.
Dismore, T.
Demers, R.
Early, M.
Felix, George
Forrester, Thomas
Fly, Peter
Fox, William
Fisher, Augustus
Grey, Thomas
Galligan, B.
Greenman, W. B.
Gould, Daniel E.
Greene, Wm. B.
Horan, John
Holmes, T. H.
Hoar, I. H.
Hart, Patrick
Hewitt, George
Higgins, M.
Haney, E.
Hanson, Hans
Hill, Edwin
Horton, B. S.
Hall, Dudley D.
Ingraham, D.
Johnson, James K.
Johnson, W. H.
Kibby, E.
Kitridge M.
Llufrio, W. B.
Larkin, James
Leavitt, Charles
Lund, Morrill
Loeffel, Augustus
Lamb, George R.
Letheran, A.
McElroy, John

Matteson, George H.
Matteson, D. E.
McCoullers, Charles
McLaughlin, Thomas
Mallon, B.
Mattison, P.
McMinnemee, M.
McMannus, James
Millard, B. F.
McGovern, John
McKenna, Charles
Mooney, Thomas
O'Sullivan, P.
Olds, Wm. K.
Pollard, John
Peck, Geo. W.
Pike, Henry
Pierson, D. B.
Powers, George A.
Pettis, George A.
Parkes, William
Rice, S. A.
Read, A. S.
Roberts, W. H.
Reynolds, P.
Ryan, Thomas
Richmond, A. C.
Santor F.
Smith, Thomas
Scannell, M.
Steele, Wm.
Smith, Francis
Sheldon, C. B.
Smith, Franklin
Slater, A. H.
Schroeer, H.
Siostien, T. V.
Sherman, C. E.
Stone, John H.
Stanley, A.
Teacher A.
Tatro, Isaac
Taylor, H. D.
Thayer R.
Von Stein, Tino
Weigel, Christopher
Williams, William C.
Whipple, P.
Warburton, James
Waters, J. F.
Warhens, E.

Witberell, B. O.

U. S. Regular Army.

Capt Jabez B. Blanding.....................21st Veteran Reserve Corps.
Lieut. J. Antoine Duvillard.........................12th U. S. Infantry.
Brevet Maj. Wm. B. Occleston.......................15th "   "
Lieut. John E. Moies.............................10th U. S. Col'd Inf.
Lieut. Frederick C. Ogden.....................1st U. S. Cavalry.
O. M. Searle...................................5th "   "
Samuel R. Bell....................................15th "   "
Dennis Wallace...................................5th U. S. Infantry.
George Watson.....................................11th "   "
F. M. Padelford.....................................12th "   "
John Charnley.....................................14th "   "
R. Swindles..14th "   "
Thomas Diamond....................................14th "   "
Christopher C. Brown..............................15th "   "
Ransom L. Smith...................................17th "   "
A. W. Beverley.....................................U. S. Signal Corps.
J. E. Elliott......................................   "   "
Gustavus H. Field..................................   "   "
C. M. Latham.......................................   "   "
S. M. Johnson......................................   "   "
William H. Seaver................................Veteran Res. Corps.

Regiments of other States.

Col. Sylvester G. Hill...............................35th Iowa.
Adjt. George F. Hodges..............................18th Mass.
Capt. Wm. T. Hodges.................................4th Mass. Cav.
Capt. F. B. Ferris..................................12th Ill.
Capt. I. D. Kenyon.................................21st Conn.
Capt. Howard Greene.................................24th Wis.
Lieut. S. H. Southwick..............................24th Ind.
William Clegg.......................................24th Ind.
——H. H. Wildman...................................16th Ill. Cav.
S. D. Wales.................................Sergt. 5th N. Y. Cav.
J. M. Parker.................................Sergt. 1st Regt.
E. J. Warren................................Sergt. 176th N. Y.
W. H. Niles...54th Mass.
A. F. Waite...15th Mass.
Corp. F. S. Grey....................................58th Mass.
Peter McDermott.....................................58th Mass.
J. B. Randall.......................................2d Mass. Cav.
George P. Read......................................2d Mass.
Richard D. Clarke................................2d Mass H. A.
J. B. Jenckes.......................................12th Mass
Benjamin J. Eddy...................................22d Mass.
D. K. Chaffee.......................................2d Mass. Cav.
A. S. Angell.......................................— Mass Regt.
William Gunn..5th Conn.
William Hough.......................................5th   "
George Lane...5th   "
William P. Clarke...................................8th   "
A. H. Greene..10th "

L. of C.

T. W. Grace...26th Conn.
Thomas S. Whitehouse.......................................15th N. Y.
J. Crocker Whitehouse......................................15th "
Charles K. Burnett ....21st "
George H. Paine..64th "
George Wheeler...61st "
J. A. Cleveland..144th "
B. J. Kilton...58th Ill.
A. E. Barber...59th Ill.
M. M. Sayles...86th Ill.
E. W. Butts..5th Ill. Cav.
Thomas A. Moore..19th Ill. Regt.
John D. Weld..— Ill. Regt.
George H. Arnold...115th Ill.
Samuel A. Eldredge...3d Minn.
C. H. Fessenden..49th Miss.
E. G. Ribley...3d Cal.
E. Kibbe...3d Cal.

Navy.

Capt. Amasa Paine,
Commander H. S. Newcomb,
Lieut. Com. Thomas P. Ives,
Lieut. Robert Rhodes,
Ass't Paymaster James H. Earle,
Act'g. 3d Asst. Eng'r. Berna Cook,
Ensign Frank G. Adams,
Act'g. Ensign F. E. Davis,
Act'g. Master Robert L. Kelly,
Master's Mate George W. Cole,
Gunner, John Myrick,
Joel B. Blaisdell,

John E. Bannon,
William A. Burlingame,
William A. Boss,
James W. Bullock,
Edgar Drowne,
Nat. C. Greene,
E. W. Goff,
William H. Horton,
P. H. Hamill,
Peter Mallahan,
L. E. Rose,
R. Sherman,

E. H. Peck.